Jordanian Political System

Jordanian Political System

Prof. Amin Al- Mashaqbeh

Professor of Political Science/ Prince Al-Hussein bin Abdullah II
School of International Studies
The University of Jordan

Former Minister of Social Development

To order additional copies of this book, contact:
Xlibris
1-888-795-4274
www.Xlibris.com
Orders@Xlibris.com
790413

Table of contents

Chapter IV

Chapter V

Index of Tables

Dedication

This book is dedicated to the new generation of Jordanians, the sons and daughters of this country.

Represented by my children:

Zaid, Miran, Lian, Dareen, Joud, and Mira

The author

Prof. Amin Al-Mashaqbeh

INTRODUCTION

First Edition:

THE AIM OF this work is to contribute to the common public awareness concerning the Jordanian political system, motivated by the belief in the value of spreading awareness regarding the political history of the Jordanian state and the defined concepts that constitute it's political system, starting with the constitutional and legal concepts which the Jordanian public authorities are built upon, and the mechanisms on which they function, in addition to the nature of their roles and functions, This book also aims to inform the citizen of the basic rights and public freedoms granted and guaranteed by the Jordanian constitution.

The main objective of this brief is to build a sound national education, and political culture for various generations, to support and deepen the concept of citizenship and boost the feelings of positive patriotism and belonging in every relevant aspect, let alone promote political loyalty to the Jordanian Hashemite regime who's roots run deep in Arab history.

This book is an attempt to shed some light on the political development of the kingdom since the early days of establishment, focused on the four Hashemite eras and what has been accomplished during those eras in terms of political stability, economic progress, social progress, and political progress, as well as to highlighting how the Hashemite dynasty has employed their religious, historical and political legitimacies alongside the public support and popular cohesion they enjoy, added to their array of achievements in sustaining

Jordan's political system despite its location in the eye of the storm and the center of events, The Jordanian system has been able to drive the country to safety through its leadership's wisdom and the support the Jordanian leadership enjoys from its people.

This book focuses on democratic development and political pluralism by looking at the evolution of parliamentary life and elections, which highlights the level of political participation, in addition to the development of political parties and the accompanying legislative development since the restoration of democratic life in 1989, and sheds light on the foundations and pillars of Jordanian foreign policy and Jordan's position on key issues in the region.

The first edition of this booklet comes to cover constitutional and legal reforms that have taken place in the Kingdom since the constitution was amended in 2011, and to also cover the issuance of a new election law No. 25 of 2012, the amendment of law No. 28 for the year 2012 and election law of 2016, the Political Parties Act of 2012, the Constitutional Court, the Independent Commission for the election Law No. 11 for the year 2012, summaries for the Royal Discussion Papers by his Majesty King Abdullah the Second, in addition to the main factors of political stability of Jordan

This attempt is an honest and effective contribution to developing national culture and to arm the new generation with knowledge and political awareness of the political history and the basic components of the Jordanian state.

We do not claim that this book complete or perfect as perfection is a trait of Allah (God) only, and therefore there must be shortcomings to this attempt, and this leaves us open to welcome any constructive criticism that aims to achieve the truth.

Author

Amin Awwad Muhanna Al-Mashaqbeh

CHAPTER I

Political History of the Hashemite Kingdom of Jordan

The establishment of the emirate:

KING FAISAL BIN Al Hussein of Syria was removed from Syria by the French in 1920, creating an opportunity for Prince Abdullah, His father's foreign minister in Hijaz, to boost army morale and mobilize the army to attack the French, Prince Abdullah arrived in Ma'an on November 5th 1920. Aiming to restore King Faisal as the king of Syria and to drive the French aggressors out of Syria.

As the British did not take any action against Abdullah's declared intentions, Prince Abdullah moved north from Ma'an. By January 1921, the word out in Karak was that Prince Abdullah was leading an army of two thousand men towards the city. [1]

Major Sir Alec Kirkbride the British counsellor in Karak welcomed Prince Abdullah to Transjordan, and soon after, Abdullah moved north up to Al Salt followed by Amman, Meanwhile in March 1921, British officials held a

---

[1]   Benjamin, Shwadran, (1959), **Jordan, A State of Tension,** NY: Council for Middle Eastern Affairs Press, P. 130.

conference in Cairo, to discuss Arab state affairs, From within that conference a decision came out allowing Prince Abdullah to stay in Transjordan as the new leader in order to organize and establish the state.

One very important turning point in the history of Transjordan was the meeting that took place between Prince Abdullah and Sir Winston Churchill in March 27th 1921, the outcome of the meeting was as follows:

1) Abdullah to prevent action against the French.
2) To renounce his rights and claims to Iraq.
3) To undertake and maintain order in Transjordan.
4) To recognize the British mandate over Transjordan as part of the Palestine mandate, and to set up an Arab government and administer the territory in the name of the mandatory.
5) To receive for six months a monthly subsidy of 5,000 British pound sterling.
6) A British representative of the High Commissioner to be stationed in Amman as adviser to the Amir's government and to help set up the administration.
7) The British to recognize the independence of Transjordan at some future date.

This agreement was beneficial to the British in two ways:

First, a central government will replace the regional local governments that failed to maintain law and order, this point has been clarified by Churchill in a speech in front of the British Parliament quoted here. "It was clear that we ought to keep order ourselves, otherwise it was difficult to deny them the right to enter and to carry out operations in our territory. On the other hand we were very reluctant to face the expense of maintaining two or three battalions in Trans-Jordanian and, worse than expense, the risk of getting them isolated and cut off by risings of the tribes. In these circumstances, we had recourse to the good offices of the Emir Abdulla, the elder brother of Emir Feisal, as part of our general policy of acting in accordance with Sherifian influence. [1]

The second benefit of the agreement is: The inauguration of a Hashemite governor in Trans Jordan, Iraq was seen by the British as a fulfilment of Britain's commitment to Sharif Hussein in return for his participation in the war against the Turks. [2]

---

[1]   Nasser, Aruri, ed, (1983), **Occupation: Israel Over Palestine,** Belmont. Mass: Association of Arab- American University Graduates, INC, P.21.

[2]   Benjamin, Shwadran. PP. 138-139

Prince Abdullah started working on a new emirate under his personal direct supervision, a task far from simple or easy given the time frame, the goals3 of prince Abdullah can be summed up as follows.

1) Abolition of local governments that existed before the arrival of Prince Abdullah.
2) Organizing a central authority in Amman as the new capital of the emirate.
3) The establishment of security and order in the territory of Transjordan.
4) Stop raids from the desert.
5) Stop groups with vengeance from attacking the French in Syria.
6) Convince different groups of people to pay taxes.

As a result, Prince Abdullah removed administrative barriers among local governments and set up acentral government under his control, The central government consisted of a board of counsellors, led by the administrative Secretary Rasheed Tuli'a, the first Jordanian Prime Minister, and on this occasion, Prince Abdullah found encouragement from the British government, and found the British government very welcoming.

On the eighteenth of April 1921, the British government appointed Julius Abramson as chief British representative in the country, and appointed seven political officers as a council for Prince Abdullah to supervise his administration.

In terms of financial support, the emirate was awarded the sum of $180 thousand pounds sterling to follow the aforementioned tasks[1], and the first Jordanian government was formed, headed by Rashid Tali'a.

The Convention signed in London in April 1923 between Britain and Transjordan made Britain recognize the autonomy of the emirate as an independent administration, and that it is separate from the administration of Palestine[2].

During that year and on the fifth of September 1923, Hassan Khalid Pasha (Abu Al Huda) formed a council called "Council of delegates" as named by Prince Abdullah and assigned the new council a new program to develop and reform in all fields.

Generally, three main forces practiced control of the country's political life in this early stage, a bureaucratical class, the British, and the tribes or clans,

---

[1] Benjamin, Shwadran. PP. 138-139

[2] P.J. Vatikiotis, (957), **Politics and Military in Jordan: (1921-1975)**, N.Y: rederic.A. Prager, PP. 44-45.

Prince Abdullah tried to maintain a balance between these powers and rule the country effectively at the same time[1].

Political Development 1921 - 1953: Political development in this period can be further divided into three sub periods, from 1921 until the Jordanian British Convention in 1928, and from 1928 until 1946, and from independence in 1946 until 1952.

The first period 1921 - 1928 was devoted to strengthen and establish the new government. The actions and measures taken by Prince Abdullah strengthened the foundations of the emirate, such as:

1) Centralizing the government under his personal control.
2) Building an army to strengthen his regime.
3) Convincing the people in general, especially the tribes to accept the presence of the new emirate.

According to Huntington, one of the most important requirements of any political system in the handling of the change is to eliminate all other local, religious and ethnic influences and to concentrate power in the national political institutions[2], For instance, Hassan Khaled, head of government from 1923 until 1926, demanded that the government organize work on establishing the greatest possible confidence and trust between the government and the people, describing the central authority as the guarantor of the rights of the taxpayer. He also pleaded for the people's support of the government and its plans.

Prince Abdullah was able to separate the administration of the Mandate in Palestine from that in Transjordan in order to prevent Jewish migrations and to have Transjordan excluded from the Balfour Declaration. However, this period of the reign of the new government was faced with great difficulties, the most difficult of which was the rebellion of some tribes, as the tribal leaders were disappointed by the presence of a central government because it would limit their control and leadership, there had been five rebellions in the country in Karak, Al Koura, Al Tafila, and Ajloun in 1921 and in Balqa (rebellion of the Al Odwan tribe) in 1923[3].

The second opponent to the emirate of the emir Abdullah was "Independence Party", a group Syrian Arab nationalist who fled Syria to escape

---

[1]   King Abdullah Ibn, Al Hussien, (1950), **The Memoirs of King Abdullah of Jordan**, London: Philosophical Library, PP. 212-213.

[2]   Samuel, Huntington, (1968), **Political Order in Changing Societies,** New Haven: Yale University Press, P. 142.

[3]   Haydar, Abidi, (1965), **Jordan: A Political study,** New Delhi: Asia Publishing ouse, PP. 13-14. Nasser, Aruri, **IBID,** P.28.

the French to Transjordan, seeking support of Prince Abdullah to help them in driving the French out of Syria. The group was then faced with the unexpected philosophy and ideas of Prince Abdullah and his way of handling such matters. The third obstacle was the Wahhabi raids of the Arabian Peninsula.

Generally Prince Abdullah succeeded in the elimination of All these movements with the help of the new army led by a British commander Frederick Beck, and according to Naseer Aruri "Not only have the British handled the issue of the opposing Independence party for Prince Abdullah, but they have also protected him from Wahhabi raids and subjected tribes who challenged him and refused to pay taxes and refused to declare loyalty to the new government[1]".

Political development after 1928:

The next period of development of the country's political system starts post 1928, before which the country was administrated and ruled with no form of constitution, up to February 20, 1928 when a British-Jordanian agreement came into effect, where Moneeb Mady and Suleiman Moosa, the authors of the book "History of Jordan" argue that the British imposed the treaty without holding any negotiations or even consulting anyone from the Jordanian side, and in any case, the British government remained in control of all relevant affairs concerning the country. Arnold Toynbee wrote the following concerning the British- Jordanian agreement: "It did not clearly recognize the independence of Transjordan to any degree beyond the technical and terminological sense of the word, similar to British treaties with leaders in the Arab gulf[2]".

The agreement contained provisions stating that Prince Abdullah must seek advice in matters relating to British budget and customs tariff, as well as foreign and military affairs. The agreement also granted the British the right to exploit natural resources in the country.

Relating to this treaty the representative of the High Commissioner of Britain was the representative of Britain in Jordan, The High Commissioner of Britain would practice the authorities given to him by this treaty through his legal adviser, his financial adviser, and the chief of department of Land.

The agreement has also given Britain the right of placing and deploying British troops, and authorized the British officer, chief of the British army(Arab Legion) judicial and administrative powers to govern the relations between clans.

---

[1]   Nasser, Aruri, **IBID**, PP.27-28. P.J. Vatikioties, **IBID**, P.47.

[2]   Nasser, Aruri, **IBID**, P.76

In the sixteenth of April 1928, and two months after the signing of the treaty, a seventy-two chapter governing law was established, based upon the British-Jordanian Agreement. In general, the law mostly served to better establish British control over the country as it is evident and apparent from most articles of the law, Following the treaty, reactions reflecting the people's disappointment were apparent, Opposition groups arranged for the first "National convention" in Amman on July 25th 1928.

The opposition came out of the convention with their demands in a document called the National Charter; the main point of the charter was to demand the establishment of an independent state in Transjordan that is a constitutional monarchy governed by Prince Abdullah and a government accountable to an elected legislature.

The document also challenged the right of the British government in overseeing the financial affairs of the country and the existence of British troops. The National Charter also requested that the government take a positive stand towards dissolving the Independence Party; Where the British officials rejected all claims under the pretext that the country was not ready for parliamentary government[1].

As we have already said, the strongest opposition to Prince Abdullah came from the Independence Party, prince Abdullah denied members of the independence party and their supporters from government posts, and issued the 1928 Nationality Act, and under this law, members of the party were not eligible for the Transjordan citizenship. Prince Abdullah also took a tough stance against the opposition, describing it as being evil and its members as being traitors[2].

However, and despite of all this, signs of political development grew as well as the public opinion, attributed to the role of political parties, and during the late 1920s and early 1930s, there were no significant political parties in the country, and there were only ideological parties being the Communist Party and the Independence party which was an Arab nationalist party.

Other parties were considered pro-government, such as the People's Party, and the Arab renaissance party. Those pro government parties promoted Prince Abdullah's objectives, the goals of the (Great Arab revolt), mainly, the unification of Greater Syria starting from Transjordan[3].

---

[1] For the Angle- Trans Jordanian Treaty in 1928, see, King Abdullah Ibn, Al Hussien, **IBID,** P.218. Benjamin, Shwadran, **IBID,** PP.167-171. Nasser, Aruri, **IBID,** PP. 76-77.

[2] Hayder, Abidi, **IBID,** PP.16-17. Nasser, Aruri, **IBID,** PP.81- 82, King Abdullah Ibn, Al Hussien, **IBID,** P.215.

[3] Hayder, Abidi, **IBID,** PP.17-18, 191-194.

Two more parties were established during the early thirties, namely, the solidarity party and the National Congress Party. In short, the political parties in Transjordan lacked programs and pulpits and outlets to contribute to the development of a sound political system[1].

As for the field of legislative development in Transjordan, the first legislative council was established in 1929 through the February 1929 elections, and was comprised of fourteen members: nine of them of Arab Muslims and three Christians and two of the Circassians, in addition to bedwin tribal leaders chosen to represent the bedwin tribes. And even though this Council had approved the agreement of 1928. (British-Jordanian treaty), it reached a deadlock upon the rejection of the annual budget.

On the ninth of February 1931, Prince Abdullah dissolved the Council. An experience that was not very encouraging for the young Emirat In sum, four legislative councils followed the first council between1931 until 1947[2].

The era of independence: The era of independence began with the Alliance held on April 25, 1946, The first article of this alliance treaty recognizes Jordan as a fully independent state, while British strategic interests were insured, in addition to handing the British government the responsibility of funding, recruiting for, and training the Arab Army (Jordanian army), Transjordan agreed to allow British troops to be based in Trans Jordanian territory and to provide all necessary assistance to facilitate their movement and to enable them. In the twenty-fifth of May 1946, The Prince of Jordan was named King of the Hashemite Kingdom of Jordan[3].

The government proposed a new constitution approved by the King on the seventh of December 1946, published in February 1947 and called for the enactment of a new electoral law provided for the creation of a bicameral parliament.

Yet, the country despite its new status, was still dependent on the British government for the development of the Arab army and its financial support[4].

---

[1] Nasser, Aruri, **IBID,** P.79.

[2] The Second Legislative council was elected in June 1931, The Third January 1934, and the Fourth in 1937. Benjamin, Shwadran, **IBID,** PP. 176, 183- 184. Nasser, Aruri, **IBID,** P. 85.

[3] King Abdullah Ibn, Al Hussien, **IBID,** P.223. Nasser, Aruri, **IBID,** P.87 Hayder, Abidi, **IBID,** P. 18.

[4] On July 7, 1946, Transjordan applied for membership in the U.N. The application was vetoed by the soviet Union, because the Soviet Union saw Transjordan a not ndependent from the British. Jordan was admitted to the U.N. On December 14,1955. Benjamin, Shwadran, **IBID,** P.215-217. Nasser, Abidi, **IBID,** P. 18.

In terms of political development during this period, the years after World War (II) marked the renewal of aspirations held during the twenties of the same century, as it appears that King Abdullah was still thinking in a Greater Syria in order to prevent the Zionist expansion, however, The British and some Arab states seemed to have concerns of the power of such a union, And not long after, king Abdullah abandoned such objectives because of the Syrian opposition, and opposition from other Arab countries, and so King Abdullah refocused his efforts on Palestine, and this older objective dates back to the mid-thirties, as in the late thirties, King Abdullah suggested that the Palestinian territory still under Arab control be merged with Transjordan, where the king was faced with opposition of many powers, including Palestinian leaderships of the Husseini family[1].

The British government was unable to resolve the problem in Palestine between the Arabs and the Jews, and hence took the case to the United nations, and In the year 1947 the United Nations decided to partition Palestine between the parties, Most Arabs in Palestine did not accept the partitioning of Palestine, and some Arab nations opposed the resolution as well.

The British government announced its intention to terminate the Mandate for Palestine and withdraw from it on May 14, 1948, and on that same day, the establishment of a Jewish state was announced, and as a result of this decision the first Arab war broke out with Israel in 1948 during which the Jordanian (Arab army) saved a part of Palestine now known as the west bank.

Termination of the mandate and the declaration of the kingdom:

Since the beginning of the British Mandate, the Prince and the people were demanding an end to the British Mandate, but the British government was rejecting the prince's demands on the grounds that the people are not yet ready for such a move, or that the international circumstances and especially World War II (1939 - 1945) would not permit. It was generally a relief to TransJordanians when Colonel Henry Fortnam Cox left leaving his post to colonel Alec Kirkbride in 1939, and even with Kirkbride demands that the mandate end. On June 27, 1945, the government of Transjordan issued a memo to the British government highlighting the end of the world war and that the time was very suitable for the independence, and demanded talks with the British in this regard.

Based on this memo, the British government invited Prince Abdullah to visit London to hold talks relating to the future of Transjordan, and consequently a

---

[1]   Area Handbook for H.K.J.1969,P.32

visit was scheduled at the beginning of year 1946, and in February 1946, Prince Abdullah, the Prime Minister, and an accompanying delegation visited London, The official visit resulted in ending the British mandate, and the recognition of the independence, alongside with a treaty of friendship and alliance between the two governments. A treaty signed on March 22, 1946, the new treaty stipulates an end to the British mandate, and the rise of a sovereign independent Transjordan, the new treaty was comprised of fourteen articles and an Annex of ten articles stating a recognition of the independence of Transjordan, a deep military alliance and diplomatic representation that the responsibility for security and defence is to be confined to the Prince, the military Annex stipulated that Britain may retain military presence in the area of Transjordan, the treaty was finalized and signed on June 17, 1946.

The people of Transjordan made the oath of allegiance to Prince Abdullah to become king and to turn the emirate into a sovereign independent kingdom, the decision was taken by the Council of Ministers on May 5, 1946, which provided for the amendment of the Basic Law and thus turned the emirate into a kingdom and was then called the Hashemite Kingdom of Jordan, and named the prince

the King of Jordan, and the declaration of independence was made with the consent of the Council of Ministers and the Legislative Council, which unanimously decided the following:

1) Declaration of the country of Jordan as a fully independent state with a hereditary parliamentary monarchy.
2) The oath of allegiance to the king, master of the country, and the founder of its existence, and heir to the Arab renaissance, Abdullah bin Al-Hussein as a constitutional monarch titled the presence of His Majesty the King of the Hashemite Kingdom of Jordan, and it was decided to designate May 25 as a day of independence.

As a result of these changes, a new constitution was required, such a constitution was established right after the declaration of independence, and was approved by the Legislative Council on November 28, 1946 and published in the Official Gazette dated February 1, 19471.

Death of the founding King:

King Abdullah Bin Al Hussein visited Jerusalem on Thursday July 19, 1951 to attend the Friday prayers in al Aqsa mosque the following day, as (God's mercy be upon him) King Abdullah had certain sentimental emotions and values to Jerusalem. On the morning of Friday, the King had paid a visit to

Ramallah and then Nablus to meet the people of those cites and inspect the citizen's needs, and returned at noon of that day to pray in al aqsa mosque, and as he entered the courtyard of the mosque, he met with crowds who came to pray, some small talk took place along with accepting people's greetings, The Jordanian royal guard battalion was obstructing the way between the king and the crowd, then the King turned his head towards Habes Al Majaly, chief of that Battalion, and said: "Don't imprison me Habes"; [1]Worth mentioning is that in Arabic, Habes means the Imprisoner.

When entering the mosque, the king refused to accompany the guards and decided to enter the mosque alone, and as he stepped into the mosque, a man held his pistol and fired to the head of the King killing him instantly at the gate of Al-Aqsa mosque, right after, the royal guard shot the shooter killing him instantly as well, On 20 July 1951, The prime ministry issued the official obituary of the martyr founder King Abdullah, who's soul had departed to god Almighty at a quarter to twelve on Friday July 20, 1951. The burial was conducted on Monday, July 23, 1951, official delegations from within the kingdom and from the other countries poured in to participate in the funeral and to pay condolences to this great loss[2].

Since the Crown Prince Talal was outside the country on a medical trip, Prince Nayef was appointed as trustee to the throne since July 20, 1951, and the trustee to the throne was sworn in front of the council of ministers and began practicing his constitutional powers since that moment.

The reign of King Talal bin Abdullah:

After recovering from his illness, Prince Talal decided to head back to the homeland Jordan, and arrived in Amman on September 6,1951, the same day he was proclaimed as the constitutional monarch of Jordan, and went to the already Held National Assembly and swore the constitutional oath, and on September 9, 1951, a Royal Decree was issued to appoint Prince Hussein bin Talal as crown prince, being the eldest son in compliance with the constitution, an amended Constitution of 1947 which was issued during the period of King

---

[1]　Suleiman, Mousa, (1968), **History of Jordan in the 20 Century,** Oxford: Oxford University Press, PP.404 - 412.

[2]　Killer is Mustafa Shukri Asho of Jerusalem, a tailor by trade, was executed at the same location, a conspiracy was unfold, and the conspirators D. Musa Abdullah Husseini, Abdelkader Farhat, Abed mahmoud akkah, and Zakaria Mahmoud Akkah who were convicted and executed on September 4, 1951 and sentenced to death in absentia was issued for Abdullah Al Tal and Musa Ahmad Ayoubi, see Suleiman Mousa, **IBID,** P.558.

Talal's reign, and it is the Constitution of 1952, this amended constitution had advanced texts in line with changes and advancements in Jordan, especially after the decision to unite the two banks (East bank and west banks of Jordan) in 1950.

Some of the achievements during this period were the Tapline agreement (Trans-Arabian Pipeline, for oil), the joint defence agreement, The pan Arab financial cooperation agreement. As a result of his lasting health condition, King Talal left Amman to Europe on May 15, 1951 for treatment and to rest, not long after, a committee of parliamentary representatives, And the king's health was not improving, Which prompted for a meeting for the national assembly on the day of August 11, 1952 to consider the medical status of king Talal, where the government laid a recommendation stating that King Talal is not able to practice his constitutional powers due to his illness, and in the second session the Council decided to terminate the rule of King Talal and calling upon Prince Hussein as the constitutional monarch of the Hashemite Kingdom of Jordan[1].

King Hussein proclaimed king of Jordan:

King Hussein arrived from London on the first week of April 1953, and was received with a big and very popular welcoming, and before receiving his constitutional powers as King of the country, made multiple visits to various regions of the Kingdom, where he had met with citizens in all parts of the country, cities, countryside, and the desert. Those visits showed a true allegiance demonstrated by the display of loyalty and popularity and sincere love.

On May 2, 1953 His Majesty was eighteen years old, and had sworn the constitutional oath before the national assembly, and on this occasion the King addressed the nation with a national and Arab national speech declaring himself as a dedicated public servant, and to announce his dedication to this country's prosperity, and to serve this homeland for the prosperity and well-being of this country and its people.

Two factors left there marks the rule of King Hussein, the first was the honouring of the royal family's legacy, protocols, and values, incorporating a strong belief in what has been handed down to him through fourteen centuries of the life of the Hashemite clan, and second is the openness to social and economical modernization, As the late king (God's mercy be upon him) was very interested in modernizing and advancing the country in all aspects. Since the early days of the kings reign, a series of events affected the political stability of the region, the widespread of Arab nationalism, effects of the cold war, the

---

[1]   Suleiman, Mousa, **IBID,** PP.561-570. James, Lent, (1990), **Hussein: biography,** P.43.

repercussions of the Arab - Israeli conflict, the Iran-Iraq war, and the second Gulf War are all events that had a direct impact on the Jordanian state, in terms of the political system, as well as the impact on people's lives, Not to mention 6 assassination attempts targeting the king in person, and regardless of all that mentioned above, King Hussein enjoyed a strong will and was perseverant, enabling him to take the Jordanian ship to the shores of safety through the above mentioned problems.

Despite all the events and storms, King Hussein was a distinguished captain, coming out of every hardship stronger than he entered it, and this sums up King Hussein throughout the years of his reign, dedicating his life to serving Jordan and the Arab case.

The death of the late King Hussein Bin Talal (1935-1999):

After intensive treatment at the (Mayo Clinic) hospital in the United States, ending with a Bone Marrow transplant. His Majesty King Hussein returned on Friday February 5, 1999 for follow-up treatment by choice and personal desire, and as a result of the treatment, and based on the medical report of his late majesty's doctors, stating the inability of the late king to carry on with his constitutional powers, the cabinet of ministers decided, based on section F of chapter 28 of the constitution, to appoint His royal highness prince Abdullah bin Al-Hussein (Bin meaning son), the Crown Prince, as a deputy for king Hussein for as long as the king's condition persists, This decision was made on the second day of the king's arrival back to Jordan, on February 2,1999.

On February 7, 1999, King Abdullah issued an obituary of His Majesty King Hussein to Jordanians, the Muslim nation, the Arab nation, and the world, An obituary stating that God had chosen the late king to his side, where his soul had departed us to join the higher God, at eleven forty three on Sunday February 7,1999.

His Majesty King Abdullah II Ibn Al Hussein:

King Abdullah Bin Al Hussein is the eldest son of the late King Hussein Bin Talal and the mother of His Majesty is Princess Muna Al Hussein, King Abdullah the second is the forty third generation to his great grandfather The prophet Mohammed peace be upon him.

King Abdullah assumed powers as the king of Jordan on Feb 7,1999, and was called King of the Hashemite Kingdom of Jordan on the twenty-first of Shawwal 1419 Hijri, corresponding to the seventh of February 1999, immediately after the death of his father, the late King Hussein Bin Talal, may God rest his soul.

King Abdullah was born in Amman on January 30,1962 and emerged under the direct supervision of the late King Hussein, King Abdullah began his education in the Islamic Educational College in Amman and continued to do so until 1966, before leaving to England and attended St Edmund's School, Hind head, Surrey, before moving on to Eagle brook School and Deerfield Academy in Deerfield, Massachusetts in the United States of America, where he finished high school. He joined the Royal Military Academy Sand Hurst in 1980, where he received military training and graduated a second lieutenant in 1981, and in October 1983 he joined the University of Oxford, where he studied international politics.

His Majesty King Abdullah II is also a naturally gifted leader, characterized by courage and bravery, and throughout his service in the armed forces, and through his participation in local and global courses, king Abdullah the second gained the traits of a professional soldier who knows what he wants, and has become the (king solder), His love for his country, His love for his people, the assistance he offers to his people, his sincerity and loyalty, his brevity and frankness, and the foresightedness are all distinctive characteristics of his personality.

His Majesty King Abdullah II inherited the religious legitimacy handed down through 14 centuries of the Mohammedian message's history, he represents the forty third generation descendants since the prophet Mohammed peace be upon him, King Abdullah also inherited the legitimacy of the Hashemite family, A legitimacy stemming from the role of the Hashemite family in leading the nation towards it's renaissance at the beginning of this century, as the Great Arab revolt led by Al shareef Hussein bin Ali (God's mercy be upon him) marked a new era of independence and liberation to the Arab nation, as the Hashemite flag and message are still held up high.

As the message and the still waiving flag are still based on the original objectives they were found for, Liberty, freedom, and unity. not to mention the political legitimacy which was founded by the late King Hussein bin Talal, may God rest his soul, political legitimacy, which means "Matching values between the political system and the values of the people" and the degree of public acceptance of the decisions of the political system." and this is quite clear in the ruling of the Hashemite family since the early days of the founding king Abdullah Ist to king Abdullah II, commander of the march into the third millennium.

From the first moment of assuming his constitutional powers, King Abdullah had the continuity of sustainable development, high among his priorities, especially economic development, combating the economic situation and countering and alleviating the country's economic debit, going forward in the economic correction plan, addressing issues of poverty and unemployment, and the attraction of foreign investors to serve the national economy, his Majesty also believes in an Arab unity at the economic front, a belief built upon his belief that the Arab nation cannot have its place among developed nations unless they have a unified position and stand on various issues, particularly the issue of economic development.

Acting upon that belief, from the moment king Abdullah came into power, he sought to activate areas of economic and trade cooperation with various Arab states, especially neighboring Arab countries.

King Abdullah confirms that he believes that there is no escape from thinking of ways and methods to meet on the points that connect Arab nations in order to come out with a formula for joint Arab cooperation and integration on the economic front, and the king also seeks to compose a formula for a future that promises integration in many areas to serve the Arab nations and their future, and this highlights the king's interest in strengthening the Jordanian-Arab, and the Arab-Arab relations.

As for His Majesty King Abdullah II vision for peace, it is based on a Just, lasting and comprehensive peace, that restores rights and achieves the aspirations of the Palestinian people in restoring their legitimate rights and establish their independent state on Palestinian national soil, and in relation to other conflicts, particularly the Syrian-Lebanese track in order to restore occupied Syrian and Lebanese territories, his Majesty finds that a just and comprehensive peace is closely tied to security and stability, and that if a just peace is not achieved, it will lead the region to despair, frustration and possibly violence, and this is why his Majesty places the international legitimacy resolutions and charters of the United Nations[1] at the utmost importance, and emphasizes on the need to achieve a two state solution.

King Abdullah II also has the legitimacy of achievement, as he has managed throughout the 13 years of his reign, to take Jordan to be among the ranks of developed countries, as his achievements have covered all aspects of life and started to touch the lives of people through which people have begun to sense the effects of development on their lives.

On Thursday, July 2, 2009 a Royal Decree was issued to appoint Prince Hussein bin Abdullah II as crown prince based on Article 28 of the Constitution.

---

[1]   See, **Journal of the Arab world**, No.1176, 09/17/1999. **Accidents magazine**,Issue 2237, September 1999. **Knight magazine**, No.140, September 1999. **The economic report**, Issue 42 June 1999.

CHAPTER II

Constitutional Development in Jordan

THE DEVELOPMENT OF the Jordanian Constitution came through three stages: the Basic Law in 1928, and the Constitution of the era of independence in 1946, which was released in 1947 and the amended Constitution of 1952, which is the Constitution currently in force. I will address the stages of development as follows:

General characteristics of the Constitution of 1928 (the Basic Law):

The "Basic Law" or the Constitution of 1928 was granted by the de-facto political power controlling the country at the time, namely, the British mandate, where the British authority gave up some of its privileges leaving space for the "Basic Law", British actions were an indicator of goals, namely, the legitimization of the Jordanian-British agreement of 1928[1],and based on the basic Law, powers were condensed into the hands of Prince Abdullah

---

[1]   There are two methods to establish two constitutions: the individual method, and the democratic method, and individual method are a grant, contract, and the grant is based on the governor's giving up of some of his powers and privileges to give the people a constitution.

bin al Hussein, where Article "16" of the law states that the legislative and administrative authorities are given to Prince Abdullah bin Al-Hussein and his heirs after him, according to the provisions of this law.

The Prince is immune from any liability and responsibility, and he is head of state that ratifies all laws, issues such laws, and monitors the implementation of laws, He also signs treaties, yet his or her Majesty the king or queen of England may intervene when necessary on behalf of Transjordan in any commercial treaty or any general international agreement. The Prince issues orders to hold elections for the Legislative Council[1].

The legislative council is subject to the power of the Monarch. He is able to call upon, suspend, or dissolve the legislative council in accordance with the provisions of law, The prince also appoints the Prime Minister, and accept his resignation, and Prince appoints all staff and dismisses them in compliance with the provisions of the law.

The basic law also states that an executive committee is to be formed from the prime minister and other members of the House of Representatives or key staff in the administration to function as an advisory committee to the prince, and it is to be noted that the executive branch of power in this basic law was an advisory role, and that will limit the role of such power or more accurately abolishes such a role[2]. As for the legislative authority, Article 25 of that law states that both the legislative counsel and the prince are responsible for legislation, the legislative council consists of publicly elected members, elected in compliance with the electoral law, which should take into account the fair representation of minorities.

As for the judiciary authority, it is an independent authority and all courts shall be free from any interference in their affairs, court judges (Both civil and sharee) are appointed by the prince, and can only be relegated in accordance with the provisions of the law on judicial authority.

General characteristics of the Constitution of 1947:

The demands of both people and government to end the British mandate paid off in Transjordan, On March 22, 1946, a treaty of friendship and alliance was signed between the two governments of Jordan and Britain, and British mandate came to an end, and as a result to that treaty, the Jordan emirate became an independent sovereign state, alongside the British declaration of the Jordanian independence, Britain retained the right to keep some troops in Transjordan, and that those troops existence was to be facilitated in return for

---

[1]   See articles 18, 19, 20 of the Basic Law.

[2]   See article 21 of the Basic Law.

grants, aid, and financial assistance to Transjordan. As a result of that treaty, on Saturday May 25, 1946 the legislative council declared The Hashemite Kingdom of Jordan and declared King Abdullah Bin Al Hussein King of Jordan.

The 1947 constitution was issued by the way of a contract between the people and the King, where the people delegate the authority and the representation of the sovereign country to the king to practice his powers in the manner offered by the people and accepted by the king.

The Constitution of 1947 used the word Constitution instead of the Basic Law as stated in the first article. The Constitution provided for the principle of independence, stating: "The Hashemite Kingdom of Jordan is an independent sovereign state and it's religion is Islam, It is a free and independent state with non-subtract able and indivisible assets."

The Constitution also stated that the system of the country is a parliamentary hereditary monarchy, and that the parliamentary government is incomplete, since the system is based on two councils, an elected council and a designated council, both executing the duties of the legislative authority, the monitoring of the legislative authority, and the monitoring of the executive authorities.

The system is also based on the existence of a leader of the country who assumes no liability, This constitution did not take into account a ministry's liability towards the parliament, but as stated in chapter 28, did take into account a ministry's liability towards the king, the constitution also states a two council system, the house of representatives and the house of senate, as well as stating that there will be a separation of powers that is an agile and not an absolute separation, the constitution of 1947 is considered one of the rigid constitutions due to the fact that special procedures are required to change the constitutional laws.

Part one: General characteristics of the Constitution of 1952:

The Jordanian Constitution of 1952 is considered an amended Constitution of the Constitution of 1947, The new constitution introduced new concepts due to the political circumstance the country was facing, most significantly the unity between the two banks of the river Jordan which was the single most influential reason for the new amendments resulting in the new constitution, Before talking about the characteristics of this constitution, we must clarify how this constitution was issued.

where one can argue that this constitution was issued by way of contract, where it is based on the political circumstance leading to the issuance of this constitution, namely the circumstance created through the unity of both banks of the river Jordan, and the previous decisions of the Jericho conference where king Abdullah bin Al Hussein was declared king over Palestine, a decision issued through the following text (The conference makes the oath of allegiance to his Majesty King Abdullah as King over Palestine), this constitution adopts the legal contractual form based on the decisions of the National Assembly of Jordan, who's members represent both the east bank and the west bank of the river Jordan, the national assembly's statement agrees to what is stated in its preamble where the preamble states that, (we Talal the first, king of the Hashemite kingdom of Jordan, under article "25" of the Constitution, and based on the decision of the Senate and House of Representatives, ratify the following amended constitution and demand it's issuance), Which makes it clear that the king's ratification came after the passing of the constitution by both the senate and the house of representatives who represent the people, which clearly demonstrates that the constitution of 1952 was issued in a contractual manner, The following are the most important characteristics of this Constitution:

1 - Jordanian people are part of the Arab nation:

Given the first Article of the Constitution, it is confirmed that (Jordan is an independent, sovereign Arab state, with unsub tractable and indivisible assets, and the Jordanian people are part of the Arab nation). completing and remedying the shortage in the law of 1947, which made no mentioning that Jordanian people are part of the Arab nation, And even though such text did not appear in the 1947 law, the fact stands that the Jordanian people are part of the Arab nation, and the 1952 text confirms and makes clear and evident that the Hashemite kingdom of Jordan is a country that is characterized by belonging to the Arab nation.

2 - Adopting the principle of the sovereignty of the nation:

Article "24" of the Constitution states that (The Nation is the source of all powers, and The Nation shall exercise its powers in the manner prescribed by the present Constitution), and you will find that such a provision was not present in previous constitutions of Jordan, and is well known that this text emphasizes the principle of the sovereignty of the people, resulting in the adoption of a democratic system, which leads to the distinction of the elected parliamentary body from other bodies in the political system.

3- Using the hereditary monarchy system and the representation system "parliamentary system"

The constitution of Jordan was issued based on the Jordanian system of a hereditary monarchy to the family of king Abdullah bin Al Hussein, where

Article (28) of the Constitution states how the throne is inherited, and the parliamentary system based on the existence of a non-liable king, an elected house of representatives, and a ministry liable before both houses of parliament, and in order to create a balance between the executive and legislative branches, the right to dissolve the national assembly was given to the executive branch of authority, and the legislative authority was given the power to withdraw the endorsement from a ministry and dissolve it.

4 – The introduction of two chambers in the composition of the legislature

The Jordanian Constitution of 1952 introduces the two chamber system in the legislature, where Article (62) of the Constitution provides that the National Assembly shall consist of two chambers: the Senate and the House of Representatives, as well as Article (63) of the Constitution stating that the Senate including the President cannot be of more than half the number of members of the House of Representatives, and the king appoints the chairman and members of the Senate, the House of Representatives on the other hand is a publicly elected council of people, elected by method of secret vote as directed by the electoral law in force in the Kingdom, each of the two chambers has specific tasks and responsibilities dictated by the constitution, the principle of equality between the two houses is taken by, yet in some areas, the house of representatives has more privileges, for example, the house of representatives is given the authority to vote on whether to endorse a ministry or a certain minister, and the authority to withdraw that endorsement and dissolve the ministry, The house of representatives can also accuse ministers, the Audit Bureau is also linked to the House of Representatives, and therefore the two chamber system helps reduce the control of any chamber over the other, in the sense that it restricts a council using the other council's authority, in addition to not rush the passing of laws by allowing the other chamber to review the outcome from the first chamber, the senate also serves to employ talents and expertise of those who do not wish to run an election or who have failed to make it to the house of representatives.

5 - Flexible separation of powers

The Jordanian Constitution of 1952 establishes the principle of the separation of the three powers as the model for state governance, where the executive branch is designated to the king and carried out by his ministers; the legislative branch was designated to the king and the national assembly, while the judiciary branch is an independent authority, and you will find that this separation is not an absolute one, as the constitution has introduced a sort of cooperation and collaboration between the executive branch and the legislative branch, characterized by that the legislative authority (national assembly) is authorized to monitor because the ministry is liable to the legislature. and may hold the ministry accountable on its works, as well as the right given to the house of representatives to endorse or withdraw an endorsement of the ministry. All the aforementioned determine the role played by the executive branch, as it is involved in the legislative process by proposing laws, endorsing laws, and issuing laws, the right to issue provisional (temporary) laws if necessary and in case a parliamentary sessions is not possible for whatever reason, the executive branch also calls for parliamentary sessions both regular and special as well as the right to delay, defer and dissolve the Council.

6- A rigid Constitution:

The Jordanian Constitution of 1952 is considered a rigid constitution, because procedures to amend or modify the constitution are not similar to procedures to amend or modify other laws and legislation, meaning there are special procedures for the process of amending constitutional laws in the Jordanian political system and these procedures are as follows:

- Granting the vote to members of the national assembly by calling them by name out loud.
- It is necessary that the draft gets a majority of two thirds of both the House of Representatives and the senate.
- The king's ratification of the draft, if the draft is not ratified by the king, this will lead to the final non-issuance of the amendment.

7 - Method of interpreting the Constitution

The Jordanian Constitution established a Constitutional Court that is an independent judicial body that stands on its own, the court consists of nine members at least, including a President, and are appointed by a Royal Decree, The term of membership to the Constitutional Court is a non-renewable six year term, and this Court is responsible for interpreting provisions of the Constitution, if requested to do so through a decision from the Council of Ministers or a decision of one of the two houses of the national assembly taken by majority vote, Interpretations are effective as soon as they are published in the Official gazette [1]. Thus the constitution makes clear how it is to be interpreted, and determines who has jurisdiction in the interpretation of rules if requested to do so, and states the authorities that can request such interpretation. The interpretation of the constitution is carried out when an argument over ambiguity arises, and the interpretation is effective upon its publication in the official gazette.

8 - Monitoring the constitutionality of laws

The Constitutional Court is responsible for overseeing the constitutionality of laws and regulations that are in force in the kingdom, and issues it's verdicts in the name of the King, and it's provisions are final and binding on all authorities and to everyone. provisions of this court are effective immediately unless a date is set for provisions to enter into force, provisions of the constitutional court are publish in the Official Gazette within fifteen days from the date they were issued.

The constitutionality of laws and regulations in Jordan can only be challenged at the constitutional court,The right to challenge the constitutionality of laws and regulations in Jordan is given directly and exclusively to both the Senators and Representatives and the Council of Ministers, and was not given directly to individuals except for cases sought out by Jordanian courts, as it is possible for any of the parties to question the constitutionality of a certain law, where the court can assess the viability of the claim, and escalate the case to the court specified by law in order to determine if it will be delegated to the constitutional court or not[2].

9 - Establishing the Audit Bureau

one of the characteristic of the constitution of 1952 is that it establishes the audit bureau to monitor the income and expenditure of the state as well as the methods and practices of financial activity, where Article 119 of the Constitution states "The audit Bureau is formed through a law, to monitor state revenues and expenditures and budgeting practices.

1 - The Audit Bureau is to present to the House of Representatives a general report includes views, comments, and statement of violations

---

[1]   See Article 57, 58 of the Jordanian Constitution amended in 1952 where it reads, the constitutional court is responsible for monitoring laws and regulations in the kingdom, and its provisions shall be final and binding on all authorities and all.

[2]   See the text of articles 58, 59, 60 of the amended Jordanian Constitution.

committed and liabilities arising from those violations, such report is presented at the start of each regular session or whenever requested by the House of Representatives to do so.

2 -   the law provides immunity for the Chairman of the Audit Bureau.

10 - Determination and regulation of rights and public freedoms

The Constitution1952 and its amendments organizes rights and public freedoms, handled in a clearer fashion than previous constitutions, as in this constitution, the entire second chapter was dedicated to organizing and establishing rights and public freedoms in the Kingdom[1].

Part Two:Constitutional amendments of the 2011:

His majesty King Abdullah II authorized a constitutional amendments for the year 2011 after the councils of senates and deputies' approval in accordance with the following:

Article 1: article no. (6) Of the Jordanian constitution is amended in accordance with the following:

Firstly: By adding the following to the the paragraph (2) with the following text and by re- numbering paragraph (2) to become paragraph (3) thereof: 2. The defence of the country, its territory, the unity of its people and the preservation Of social peace are sacred duty of every Jordanian.

Secondly: by adding paragraphs (4) and (5) to it with the following two texts: 4. The family is basis of society the core of which shall be religion, morals, and Patriotism; the law shall preserve its legitimate entity and strengthen its ties and values.5. The law shall protect motherhood, childhood, and the old-aged; and shall avail care for the youngsters and those with disabilities, and protect them against abuse and exploitation.

Article 2: amendment of article (7) of the constitution by considering its paragraph (1) and adding paragraph (2) to it with the following text: 2- Every infringement on rights and public freedoms or the inviolability of the Private life of Jordanians is a crime punishable by law.

Article 3: the text of article (8) is declined from the law and replaced by the following text:

Article 8: 1. No person may be seized, detained, imprisoned or the freedom thereof restricted except in accordance with the provision of the law.2.

---

[1]   For more detail, see the second part of Chapter III.

Every person seized, detained, imprisoned or the freedom therof restricted should be treated in a manner that preserves human dignity; may not be tortured in any manner, bodily or morally harmed; and may not be detained in other than the places permitted by laws; and every statement uttered by any person under torture, harm or threat shall not be regarded.

Article 4: with adding the phrase (be prevented from movement) after the phrase (a party) in the text the paragraph (2) from article (9) in the constitution is modified.

Article 5: Article (15) of the constitution is adjusted in accordance to the following: Firstly: with adding paragraph (2) to the following text: 2. The state shall guarantee the freedom of scientific research and literary, technical, cultural and sports excellence provided that such does not violate the provisions of the law order and morality.3. The state shall guarantee the freedom of the press, printing, publication and information media within the limits of the law.4. Newspaper and information media may not be suspended nor the license therof revoked except by a judicial; order in accordance with the provisions of the law.

Secondly: by re numbering the paragraphs from (2) to (5) to become from (3) to (6) respectively.

Article 6: Adding the phrase (unions) after the word (societies) in the two paragraphs (2) and (3) article (16) of the constitution which is amended.

Article 7: Article (18) of the constitution is declined and replaced by the following text:

Article18: All postal and telegraphic correspondence, telephonic communications and the other means of communication shall be regarded as secret and shall not be subject to censorship, viewing, suspension or confiscation except by a judicial order in accordance with the provisions of the law.

Article 8: By deleting the word (primary) and replace it with the word (basic), article (20) is amended.

Article 9: with adding the word (independent) after the phrase (The Judicial power), article (27) is amended.

Article 10: Article (42) of the Constitution shall be declined and replaced by the following text:

Article 42: No person shall hold the position of Minister and the like except a Jordanian who does not hold the nationality of another state.

Article 11: with phrase (another legislative) cancellation and replacing it by the word (law), the paragraph (1) of the article (45) of the constitution is amended.

Article 12: the text of article (50) is declined from constitution and replaced by the following text:

Article 50: In the event of the resignation, dismissal or death of the Prime Minister, all Ministers shall be considered as having necessarily resigned.

Article 13: article (45) of the constitution is amended as follows:

Firstly: with the phrase cancellation (If the Council is not held or dissolved, The Throne speech is considered a ministerial statement for the purpose of this article)1

Secondly: by cancellation of the phrase (and if the council wasn't conducted or over so the speech of the throne is considered a minister statement for the purposes of this article)[1] contained in paragraph.

Thirdly: by adding the paragraphs (4), (5), and (6) with the following text: 4. If the House of Representatives is not in session, it shall be called to convene in an extraordinary session, and the council of Ministers shall place its Mnisterial statement and request the vote of confidence on that statement within a month of the date of its formation. 5. If the House of Representatives stands dissolved the council of Misnisters shall place its ministerial statement and request the vote of confidence on that statement within a month From the date of the convening of the new House. 6. For the purposes of the paragraphs (3), (4), and (5) of this article The Council of Ministers shall obtain the vote of confidence if the absolute majority of members of the House of Representatives vote favorably for it.

Thirdly: renumbering the two articles (54) and (53) of the constitution to become the two articles (53) and (54).

Article 14: the text of the article (55) is cancelled from the constitution and replaced by the following text:

Article 55: Ministers shall be tried for crimes attributed to them resulting from the performance of their functions before the competent civil courts in the capital, in accordance with the provisions of the law.

Article 15: the text of article (56) of the constitution is declined and replaced by the following text:

Article 56: The House of Representatives shall have the right to refer the Ministers ti the Attorney General along with stating the justifying reasins. The decision of referral shall not be issued except by the majority of the members of whom the House of representatives is composed.

Article 16: the text of article (57) is cancelled from constitution and replaced by the following:

---

[1]   Contained in paragraph 3

Article 57: The Minister who shall be accused by the Attorney General upon issuances of the decision of referral by the House of Representatives shall be suspended from office; his resignation shall not prevent the institutions of proceedings against him nor the continuation of his trial.

Article 17: the constitution is amended as the following: Firstly: by adding (the fifth unit) before article (58) by the title: **Constitutional Court:** Secondly: to become from (the sixth) to (tenth) respectively by renumbering the chapters from (fifth) to (ninth).

Article 18: the text of the articles (58), (59), (60), (61) of the constitution and replaced by the following text:

Article 58: 1. A Constitutional Court shall be established –by a law- the headquarters of which shall be in the Capital; shall be considered as an independent and separate judicial body; and shall be composed of nine members at least inclusive of the President, to be appointed by the King.2- The term of membership in the Constitutional Court shall be six years non-renewable.

Article 59: The Constitutional Court shall have the competence of oversight on the constitutionality of the applicable laws and regulations and its judgments shall be issued in the name of the King; its judgement shall be final and binding on all authorities and on all; its judgment shall as well be effective immediately unless the judgement specifies another date for its effectiveness; the judgments of the Constitutional Court shall be published in the official Gazette within fifteen days of the date of issuance. The Constitutional Court shall have the right to interpret the provisions of the Constitution if such is requested therefrom by a decision issued by the Council of Ministers or by a decision taken by wither House of the Parliament by majority; its decision shall be effective after its publication in the Official Gazette.

Article 60: The following entities- for limitation- shall have the right to directly challenge at the Constitutional Court the constitutionality of the applicable laws and regulations: The Senate, The House of Representatives and The Council of Ministers. In the case viewed by courts, amy of the parties of the case may raise the issue of the non-constitutionality; the court shall it finds that the plea is serous- refer it to the court specified by the law for the purposes of the determination of its referral to the Constitutional Court.

Article 61: A member of the Constitutional Court shall meet the following conditions: To be Jordanian and not hold the nationality of another state. To have reached fifty years of age. To be of those who served as judges in the court of Cassation and the High Court of Justice, or of the professors of law in universities who hold the rank of professor; or of the lawyers who spent a period of not less than fifteen years in the practice of laws ; and the specialists to whom the conditions of membership in the Senate apply.

Article 19: Text of article (67) of the constitution is cancelled and replaced by the following text:

Article 67: 1. The House of Representatives shall be composed of members elected by general, secret and direct election in accordance with an election law which shall ensure the following matters and principles: a. The right of candidates to observe the electoral process. b. The punishment of those adversely influencing the voters' will. c. The integrity of the electoral process in all of its stages. 2. A law shall establish an independent body to manage the parliamentary and municipal elections, as well as any other general elections, in accordance with the provisions of the law. The Council of Ministers may assign the independent body to manage or supervise any other elections at the request of the entity authorized by law to conduct such elections.

Article 20: Text of constitution article (71) is cancelled and replaced by the following text:

Article 71:

1) The Judiciary shall have the competence to determine the validity of the election of the members of the House of Representatives. Every voter from the constituency shall have the right to file a petition to the Court of Appeal which has jurisdiction over the constituency of the representative the validity of whose election is contested from his constituency within fifteen days from the date of the publication of the elections results in the Official Gazette indicating therein the reasons of his petition; its decisions shall be final and not subject to any way of challenge; its judgments shall be issued within thirty days from the date of the registration of the petition thereat.

2) The Court shall resolve either to reject the petition or to accept it in terms of subject; in which case it shall announce the name of the successful representative.

3) The House of Representatives shall announce the invalidity of the membership of the representative who the Court invalidated his membership and the name of the successful representative effective from the date of the issuance of the judgment.

4) The actions taken by the member whose membership was invalidated by the Court prior to its invalidation shall be deemed correct.

5) Should it be evident to the Court - as a result of its consideration of the petition filed thereto - that the election procedures in the constituency to which the petition relates are not consistent with the provisions of

the law, it shall issue its decision for the invalidation of the election in that constituency.

Article 21: constitution article (73) is amended by cancellation of paragraph (4), (5), and (6) included therein.

Article 22: Text of article (74) of the constitution is cancelled and replaced by the following text: **Article 74: Article 74**

1) If the House of Representatives is dissolved for any reason, the new House may not be dissolved for the same reason.

2) The government - in the tenure of which the House of Representatives is dissolved - shall resign within a week from the date of dissolution; and its head may not be designated to form the government that follows.

3) The Minister who intends to nominate himself for elections shall resign sixty days at least prior to the election date.

Article 23: article 75 of the constitution is amended in accordance with the following:

Firstly: By cancellation of item (B) of paragraph (1) thereof and to be substituted by the following text: B- Who holds the nationality of another state.

Secondly: By cancellation of item (O) of paragraph (1) thereof and re-numbering the two items (Z) and (H) listed therein to become (O) and (Z) thereof respectively.

Thirdly: by cancellation the text of paragraph (2) thereof and replacing it by the following text: 2. Every member of the Senate and the House of Representatives - during the term of his membership - shall refrain from contracting with the government; public official corporations; the companies owned or dominated by the government; or any public official corporation whether this contracting is in a direct or indirect way with the exception of contracts of lease of land and property and who is a shareholder in a company the members of which exceed ten persons.

Fourthly: by adding paragraph (3) thereto with the following text: 3- If any of the cases of disqualification provided for in Paragraph (1) of this Article takes place as regards any of the members of the Senate and the House of Representatives during his membership or appears after his election, or violates the provisions of Paragraph (2) of this Article, his membership shall necessarily be non-existent and his seat shall become vacant, provided that the decision - if issued by Senate - shall be submitted to His Majesty the King for ratification.

36 **Article 24**: The paragraph (3) of article (78) of the constitution is amended by the phrase (four months) an (the four months) coming therein cancellation and replaced by the phrase (six months) and the phrase (the first six months). 3. The ordinary session of the Parliament shall begin on the date upon which it is summoned to meet in accordance with the two preceding Paragraphs, and this ordinary session shall last for six months, unless the King dissolves the House of Representatives before the expiration of that period. The King may prolong the ordinary session for another period not exceeding three months for the completion of pending matters. At the expiration of the first six months or any prolongation thereof, the King shall prorogue the said session.

Article 25: The constitution article (84) paragraph (1) is amended by phrase (four months) and (the four months) coming therein cancellation and replaced by the following text: No meeting of either of the two Houses shall be considered duly constituted unless attended by the absolute majority of the members of the House, and shall continue to be duly constituted as long as this majority is present therein.

Article 26: Constitution article (88) text is cancelled and replaced by the following text:

Article 88: If the seat of a member of the Senate and the House of Representatives becomes vacant by death, resignation or any other reasons with the exception of whoever a judicial decision was issued in his regards invalidating his membership, the relevant House shall notify the Government or the Independent Election Commission - if he is a representative - within thirty days from the vacancy of the seat of the member; and his seat shall be filled by appointment if he is a Senator or in accordance with the provisions of the Election Law if he is a representative within a period of two months from the date of the notification by the House of the vacancy of the seat; and the membership of the new member shall last to the end of the term of the House.

Article 27: Text of paragraph 1 of article 89 of constitution is cancelled and replaced by the following text: In addition to the circumstances in which the Senate and the House of Representatives hold meetings pursuant to Articles (29), (34), (79) and (92) of this Constitution, they shall jointly meet at the request of the Prime Minister.

Article 28 : text of article 94 of constitution is cancelled and replaced by the following text:

Article 94 1. When the House of Representatives is dissolved, the Council of Ministers - with the approval of the King - shall have the right to issue provisional laws to cover the following matters:

a) General disasters.
b) The state of war and emergencies.
c) The need for necessary and urgent expenditures which cannot be postponed.

The provisional laws - which should not violate the provisions of the Constitution - shall have the force of law, provided they are placed before the Parliament in the first sitting it holds. The Parliament shall take decisions in their regards during two consecutive ordinary sessions from the date of their referral. It may approve, amend or reject such laws. If it rejects them or the period provided for in this Paragraph elapses without decisions, the Council of Ministers should - with the approval of the King - declare their nullity immediately; and from the date of such declaration the force of law they had shall cease provided that this shall not affect contracts or acquired rights.

2. Provisional laws shall come into effect in the manner laws come into effect by virtue of the provision of Article (93) of this Constitution.

Article 29: paragraph (1) Article (98) of the Constitution shall be amended after what is stated therein and by adding the two paragraphs (2) and (3) to it by the following two texts: 2. A Judicial Council shall - by a law - be established to assume all the affairs relevant to civil judges. 3. Without prejudice to Paragraph (1) of this Article, the Judicial Council shall solely have the right to appoint civil judges in accordance with the provisions of the law.

Article 30: By the cancellation of the phrase "Supreme Court of Justice" contained therein and to replace it by the words "administrative district in two degrees",

Article (100) is amended by the constitution.

Article 31: The text of article (101) is cancelled and replaced by the following text:

Article 101:

1) The courts shall be open to all and shall be immune from interference in their affairs.
2) No civilian may be tried in a criminal case where all its judges are not civilian, the exception to that are the crimes of treason, espionage, terrorism, the crimes of drugs and currency forgery.
3) Court sittings shall be public unless the court decides that they be in camera in consideration of public order or in preservation of morals. In all cases, the pronouncement of the verdict shall be in a public sitting.
4) The accused is innocent until proven guilty by a final verdict.

Article 32: text of paragraph (2) of article (109) of constitution is cancelled and replaced by the following text: The Tribunals of Religious Communities shall apply the procedures and provisions related to the matters of personal status which are not considered matters of personal status of Moslems within the jurisdiction of the Sharia Courts; provided that the legislations of such Tribunals shall organize the conditions of the appointment of their judges and the procedures of trials before them.

Article 33: Text of paragraph (1) of article (112) of constitution is cancelled and replaced by the following text:

1. The General Budget draft law and the Governmental Units Budgets draft law shall be submitted to the Parliament at least one month before the beginning of the fiscal year for their consideration in accordance with the provisions of the Constitution. The same provisions related to the Budget in this Constitution shall apply to them. The Government shall submit the final accounts by the end of six months from the end of the previous fiscal year.

Article (34): Text of paragraph (1) of article (119) of constitution is cancelled and replaced by the following text: 1. The Audit Bureau shall submit to the Senate and the House of Representatives a general report containing the irregularities committed, the liability resultant therefrom, its opinions and comments at the beginning of every ordinary session and whenever either House requests it to do so.

Article (35): Article (122) of constitution is cancelled and replaced by the following text:

Article 122:

1) A High Tribunal shall be composed of the Speaker of the Senate, as President, and of eight members: three of whom shall be appointed by the Senate from its members by ballot, and five from the judges of the highest civil court in the order of seniority; and when necessary, the number shall be completed from the presidents of the courts that follow it in the order of seniority as well.

2) The High Tribunal shall have the right to interpret the provisions of the Constitution if it is so requested by a decision issued by the Council of Ministers or by decision taken by either House of Parliament by absolute majority; and shall be effective after its publication in the Official Gazette.

3) This Article shall be considered as necessarily null and void once the Constitutional Court law is put into effect.

CHAPTER III

Jordanian political system

Parliamentary system:

THE PARLIAMENTARY SYSTEM in Jordan is based on cooperation and balance of power, especially the executive and legislative branches, and is known as the system based on equality between the two branches of the state "the parliament and the government", Where no authority dominates or dictates the other. The parliamentary system relies on two main pillars: the dual composition of the executive branch and mutual cooperation between the executive and legislative branches.

1. The dual composition of the executive branch:

The executive power in a parliamentary system consists of the highest head of state and the ministry, and the first part of this power is the head of state, which can be a king or a President of a Republic depending on the nature of the existing political system. The participation of the Head of State with the Ministry in governance is not inconsistent with the nature of the parliamentary system, provided the existence of a ministry should be able to take responsibility in return for the intervention of the head of state in governance matters[1].

The second part of the executive branch in the parliamentary system is the ministry consisting of the Prime Minister as Chairman and a group of ministers as needed and as dictated by public interest of the state. They meet in a single Council called the council of ministers to set the policy for a government, and a ministry in this system is considered the effective device accountable to the parliament in shared accountability for the entire body of Ministers or as individual ministers responsible and liable separately.

The head of state whether King or president is entitled to appoint the Prime Minister and Ministers, but this entitlement is not absolute, as in countries where the state is multi-party political system, the king or president must appoint the leader of the party that has managed to win the majority of seats in parliament, or the head of a coalition of parties if that is the case, this is because the government or ministry must obtain the parliament's endorsement if the ministry is to come into power and sustain the endorsement.

2. Cooperation and balance between the executive and legislative branches:

Parliamentary systems are based on the principle of separation of powers, yet that separation of powers is not absolute, there is also cooperation and balance between the legislative and the executive branch, as an example of such cooperation between the two branches is that the executive branch carries the tasks related to composing the parliament such as setting the dates for a public election and arranging for that election, and calling for parliamentary to convene, also, The head of state carries out the opening of the regular sessions, and the executive branch has the right to end a session or postpone it. The executive branch also helps in proposing laws, approving laws, and issuing laws, and the authority to create governmental regulations. The executive branch can also dissolve parliament, where this means the ending for Parliament before the end of its legal term, which is considered one of the most effective means of monitoring by the executive branch over the legislative branch. On

---

[1] Political researcher Bordeaux sees that parliamentary systems are based on equality between powers and others find that due to the evolution and advancement of such systems, equality between the branches is no longer real, and only applies in theory, as researcher Horiu finds that the executive branch has overpowered the legislator, see Anwar, al-Khatib, (1970), **the state and the constitutional systems**, Edition2, Beirut, PP.128. See Abdel Moneim Mahfouz, (1987), **the principles of the political systems**, Amman, P.282.

the other hand, the executive branch is responsible in front of the legislative branch through the liability of the ministry[1], The legislative branch also has some powers that are of the executive branch's domain, denoting the existing cooperation between the two powers, such as the monitoring of political affairs and financial affairs through the right to pose questions, carry out investigations, and the ability to accuse members of the executive branch. as the principal of the collective and the individual liability of ministers is a weapon used by the legislative branch against the executive branch. As the legislative branch can withdraw the endorsement from the ministry, and in that case, the government resigns.

The principle of ministerial responsibility is the weapon that is meant to balance and counter the executive Branch's ability to dissolve parliament, but this right, which is a cornerstone of all parliamentary systems has been compromised by the constitutional amendments of 2011, as the amendment of Article74 requires that when the house of representatives is dissolved, the government must resign within a week of that date of dissolution, and it's prime minister may not be assigned the following ministry as Prime Minister. What this means is that a cornerstone of the parliamentary system concerning the desolation of the house of representatives has been restricted, and consequentl disturbing the balance between the branches, giving the legislative branch an advantage at the expense of the executive branch's authority. As mentioned before, parliamentary systems are based on the principle of balance between powers. On one hand, the executive branch has the right to dissolve the House of Representatives provided they offer a reason for the dissolution. On the other hand,the legislature has the right to withdraw the endorsement of the government. The condition stated in article 74 paragraph "2" has compromised a cornerstone of that system, therefore it is very important that the text is restored to what it has been before this amendment. It is also advised to abolish the requirement in paragraph "2" of Article 74 as the legislative branch has armed itself with a law that would punish a government in case the House of Representatives was dissolved by ending that government within a week. The harsher condition or requirement lies is the inability of the head of government to form the next government and this also restricts the king's authority against the 35th provision of the constitution.

The constitutional amendments in 2012 ended the state predominance of the executive branch over the legislative, and turned the predominance in favour of the legislative branch at the expense of the executive branch. The reason behind this is that the project aiming to amend the constitution did

---

[1]   Ibrahim, Shiha,(1981), **contemporary political systems: states and governments**, Beirut, PP.217 - 219.

not take in mind the public good and higher interest of the state as much as it was concerned in limiting the executive branch's powers with no regard to the principle of balance between political powers.

In general one can summarize the most important characteristics of a parliamentary system based upon the principle of cooperation and balance between the authorities and based on the flexible separation of power as follows:

1) Head of State is not responsible or liable.
2) The Ministry is responsible to Parliament.
3) The ministry must get the endorsement of parliament to be allowed to carry out its duty.
4) The ministry should be homogeneous, supposedly of the same party that holds a majority in parliament.
5) The ministry has the right to request the dissolution of parliament from the Head of State in cases parliament does not cooperate, a right countering the parliament's right to withdraw the endorsement of the ministry[1].

The Executive branch:

The executive branch of government can be defined as a political organization with wide discretionary powers with the purpose of overseeing the implementation of laws and regulations, and to represent the state in its international and military relations.

The executive branch includes the prime minister and his ministers and advisors, alongside heads of the branches of various institutions, representing the real organization of the State in the form of President and Council[2].

In most countries of the world and especially those with parliamentary systems, we find that the executive branch is divided into two parts, namely the head of state and head of government and since the Jordanian political system is a parliamentary monarchy, where the king is head of state and the prime minister is head of government. The Ministry or the Council of Ministers

---

[1] For more details on regulations, see Yahya, Al-Jamal, (1970), **Contemporary Political System,** Cairo, PP.171-176. Abdel Moneim, Mahfouz, **IBID,** PP.79- 286. Anwar, al-Khatib, (1970), **State and Constitutional System,** Edition2, Beirut, PP.125-148. Ibrahim, Shiha, **IBID,** PP.217-223, the amendment of Article 74, paragraph "2" in breach of the principle of balance between the authorities

[2] Raymond, Dioctyl, (1963), **Political Science,** Part II, (translation of Fadel Zaki), Baghdad, PP.114-115. Gainble Jr,. John King, (1983), **Introduction to Political Science,** P.232.

(cabinet) is considered an executory body with powers allowing that body to take political, social, and economical decisions concerning the state's general policy, and the government in general. "The Prime Minister and Ministers" work as a single unit to achieve the general policy of the state. It represents the structure containing the executory devices and managerial activities that execute the government's tasks, this structure is called a bureaucracy, which is a rational system or a rational structure or an organized structure designed to efficiently carry the general policy. For that purpose, a bureaucracy works through a fixed set of rules and regulations belonging to a hierarchy of authority, and generally, the executive branch specializes in carrying out general policies set forth in the state, and works to secure the rule of law, set by the legislative authority and supported by judiciary authority. The duties of this power requires proficiency in administrative duties, and quickness in the execution of decisions, resolute action, and a wise consistent policy, in order to conduct government tasks, and provide service to citizens, as well as to achieve the highest degree of relative justice.

The executive branch in the Hashemite Kingdom of Jordan:

Executive power in the Jordanian political system is represented by the King, who practices this authority through his ministers in accordance with the provisions contained in the Jordanian Constitution[1]. The king is the head of state, and represents the state, and the executive power is assigned to him and to the Council of Ministers consisting of the chief minister (Prime Minister) or also called the head of government, and a set number of ministers set in accordance to the circumstances and as required by the public interest.

Head of State; The King:

The Jordanian Constitution states that the political system in the Hashemite Kingdom of Jordan is a representative, hereditary parliamentary monarchy. and monarchy is the oldest form of government in history, where this system developed alongside the evolution and fundamental changes in government and means of governance, What is meant by a monarchy is a system where the head of state obtains his right to rule by inheritance, and is known as king, and the state as Kingdom, and in this century, there are three types of monarchies, absolute monarchy, restricted monarchy, and the modern constitutional monarchy, The Jordanian monarch is a mix between a restricted monarchy and a modern constitutional monarchy, where the states relies on the people

---

[1]   Article26 of the Jordanian Constitution.

who are the source of powers, and the ultimate source of legitimacy, and the king is the head of state and the symbol of the continuity of government and resembles the national identity and national unity[1].

The throne of the Kingdom is hereditary in a family of King Abdullah Bin Al Hussein, And the throne is inherited by male offspring of the king in accordance with the following provisions[2]:

a) *The Royal title shall pass from the holder of the Throne to his eldest son, and to the eldest son of that son and in linear succession by a similar process thereafter. Should the eldest son die before the Throne devolves upon him, his eldest son shall inherit the Throne, despite the existence of brothers to the deceased son. The King may, however, select one of his brothers as heir apparent. In this event, title to the Throne shall pass to him from the holder of the Throne[3].

b) Should the person entitled to the Throne die without a male heir, the Throne shall pass to his eldest brother. In the event that the holder of the Throne has no brothers, the Throne shall pass to the eldest son of his eldest brother. Should his eldest brother have no son, the Throne shall pass to the eldest son of his other brothers according to their seniority in age[4].

c) In the absence of any brothers or nephews, the Throne shall pass to the uncles and their descendants, according to the order prescribed in paragraph (b) above[5].

d) Should the last King die without any heir in the manner prescribed above, the Throne shall devolve upon the person whom the National Assembly shall select from amongst the descendants of the founder of the Arab Revolt, the late King Hussein Ibn Ali[6].

---

[1] Ameen, Al-Mashaqbeh, (1988), **Political modernization and political stability in Jordan**, Amman: Dar aljeel, Beirut: Addar al arabeyeh, PP.117-178. About contemporary monarchy types, see Ahmed, Attia, (1972), **Political dictionary,** Renaissance House Press, PP.1219-1221. Austin,
Ranney, (1975), **The Governing Of Men**, Illinois: Dryden Press, P.38. Robert, Cord and Kay, Lawson, (1985), **The Human Polity,** Boston: Mass Press, P 347.

[2] Article 28 of the Constitution of Jordan.

[3] Article 28 of the Constitution, paragraph A, under the amendment dated 01/04/1965

[4] Article 28 of the Constitution, paragraph (b).

[5] Article 28 of the Constitution, paragraph (c).

[6] Article 28 of the Constitution, paragraph (d).

The conditions to be provided by those who ascend the throne (The King):

1) To be a Muslim.
2) Should be mentally sound.
3) Born to a legitimate wife.
4) Born to Muslim parents.
5) No person shall ascend the Throne who has been excluded from succession by a Royal Decree on the ground of unsuitability. Such exclusion shall not of itself include the descendants of such person[1].
6) The King attains his majority upon the completion of his eighteenth year according to the lunar calendar.
7) The King shall upon his succession to the Throne take an oath before the National Assembly, to respect and maintain the Constitution and be loyal to the nation.

The King's Viceroy/ vice-regent:

Should the King wish to leave the country, he shall, before his departure and by a Royal Decree, appoint a Vice-regent or a Council of Vice-regents to exercise his powers during his absence. The Vice-regent or Council of Vice-regents shall observe any conditions which may be prescribed in the Royal Decree. If the absence of the King is extended to more than four months and the National Assembly is not in session, the Assembly shall be summoned immediately to consider the matter[2].

A deputy committee is assembled in the case where the king is unable to take over his duties due to illness, the deputy or deputy committee is assigned with a royal decree, and in the case of the king's inability to issue a royal decree, the council of ministers shall, after verifying the king's inability, immediately convene the National Assembly to look into the matter. And if absolute evidence of an illness that deems the king incapable of carrying his tasks is found, the national assembly can terminate the king's reign and the thrown is handed to the rightful person in accordance with the constitution. if the National Assembly is dissolved at such a time, and a new assembly has not yet been elected, the previous council is convened to consider this matter[3].

---

[1] Article 28, Royal decree must be signed by the Prime Minister and four ministers at least, including the Minister of the Interior and Justice.

[2] Article 28 of the Jordanian Constitution paragraph (I).

[3] Article 28 of the Jordanian Constitution paragraph (M).

The deputy (Viceroy) must take an oath before the council of ministers to maintain and honor the constitution, and to be faithful to the nation, prior to the taking up of the king's duties[1].

The Vice-regent must be no less than thirty lunar years of age, yet, a male member of the royal family may be appointed provided that he has completed eighteen lunar years of age, In the case the Vice-regent dies, the council of ministers must appoint a successor to the Vice- regent[2].

Regency Council and conditions of regency:

In the case where the thrown is handed down to a crown prince who has not completed eighteen lunar years, duties and power of the king are practiced by a Regency council, appointed by with a royal decree from the former king, and if the former king was deceased without appointing a Regency Council, the council of ministers may appoint the Regency Council.

The Regency Council shall exercise the powers of the king excluding the modification of any provisions of the constitution relating to the king's inherited rights, the Regency and all members of a Regency council must be over 30 lunar years of age, yet it is permissible to appoint a male member of the royal family provided that he has completed 18 lunar years of age as either a regency or a member of a regency council, and before entrusting the regency or regency council to their tasks, the constitutional oath of honoring the constitution and to be faithful to the nation must be sworn in before the council of ministers. In the case where a member of the Regency Council or a regency dies or becomes incapable of carrying his tasks or duties, the council of ministers is entitled to name a fitting person to carry his responsibilities[3].

A king's position in the Jordanian political system:

In terms of the political system in Jordan, the position of the king is defined by the constitution as stated in article 30, stating that the king is the head of the state, and is immune from all consequences and liability, and the king carries out all of his authorities granted to him by the constitution with the existence of a ministry liable in before the general assembly. The king carries his authorities by issuing royal decrees, a decree is signed by the prime minister and the relevant

---

[1]   Article 28 of the Constitution paragraph (Y) in addition to Article 29 of the Constitution.

[2]   Article 28 of the Jordanian Constitution.

[3]   Article 28 of the Constitution, paragraph (K).

minister or ministers, and the king's approval is given by signing above the other signatures mentioned above[1].

The Jordanian constitution has specified that the king's oral or written commands do not indemnify ministers from their responsibilities, as ministers and the prime minister are collectively liable before the house of representatives over the policy of the government, in addition to every minister being personally liable to the house of representatives for tasks carried out by his ministry[2].

The king's rights:

As mentioned, the king in the Jordanian political system is the head of state, and is immune from all consequences and liability; the king is also head of the executive branch, power that he exercises through his ministers. The executive authority has a range of competencies, administrative, political, and legislative competencies; the king practices his constitutional authority as head of state and head of the executive branch of power[3].

The King in the Jordanian political system exercises his powers through the ministry because the ministry is responsible and liable before the House of Representatives for all work performed by the King, yet the king exercises his rights alone without the involvement of the ministry, this is because of legal and political considerations, in this part we will talk about the rights of the king in the Jordanian political system as set out by the Jordanian Constitution, rights include legal, political and administrative rights namely:

a) The right to command the armed forces: The king is considered head of state and head of the executive branch and being responsible for security and political stability, as well as internal stability, it is normal that he would be given the higher command of the Jordanian army, as the Constitution of the Hashemite Kingdom of Jordan states that the king is the supreme commander of the ground forces, navy and air force. The King exercises this right through his Chiefs of the "general command", supervising, directing, and guiding for development of the

---

[1] Article 40 of the Jordanian Constitution, and this article specifies that the royal decree is must first be signed by the prime minister and the relevant minister or ministers, then the king signs his approval above the other signatures.

[2] Article 49 and Article 51 of the Jordanian Constitution.

[3] Adel, Hiyari, (1972), **Constitutional Law: Jordanian Political System,** Amman, PP.684-685.

armed forces and their function[1] in both normal and extraordinary circumstances.

b) The right to appoint the cabinet and to dissolve it.

The executive power in Jordan is tied to the king and exercised through the king's ministers, and as the head of the executive branch, the king appoints the prime minister and dismisses him and accepts his resignation. The king appoints the ministers and remove them and accepts their resignation based on the recommendations of the Prime Minister[2]. The king's right to appoint a prime minister is a personal right and is executed by him directly through a royal decree. as for the appointment, dismissal, and accepting the resignation of ministers, the decree is issued in based upon recommendations of the prime minister and the approval of the king, and therefore ministers are appointed and dismissed through a royal decree signed by both the prime minister and the king[3].

c) The right to appoint members of the Senate:

The Legislative authority in the Hashemite Kingdom of Jordan consists of two chambers, one is the elected House of Representatives and the other is the appointed Senates, and the appointment of members of the Senate is done by the King through a royal decree, signed by the Prime Minister and the Minister of Interior. The head of senate is chosen from among the member of the senate with a royal decree signed by his Prime Minister and the Minister of the Interior as stated in Article 36 by saying the King appoints members of the Senate and appoints the Speaker from amongst them and accepts their resignation[4].

d) The right to form and give ranks and decorations of various kinds:

The King in the Jordanian political system creates and confers and withdraws civil and military ranks and medals and honorific titles. He may delegate this authority to others through a special law[5], The king

---

[1] Article 32 of the Jordanian Constitution

[2] Article 35 of the Jordanian Constitution.

[3] In the constitutional amendment of 2011 and in the second paragraph of Article 74, the king has been restricted not to appoint the last prime minister that has had his ministry dissolved due to the desolation of the House of Representatives.

[4] Article 36 of the Jordanian Constitution.

[5] Article 37 of the Jordanian Constitution, paragraph 1 of the second paragraph of this article about currency states that (money on various kinds of paper or metal, is casted and carved and printed in the name of His Majesty the King), where the second paragraph of Article 37 states that the currency is carved and printed in the King's name to implement the law.

may exercises this right to establish and grant ranks whether military or civilian, through the ministry but given personally by his Majesty the King.

e) The right to appoint the courtiers and the palace staff:
Of the kings personal rights is the right to appoint courtiers and palace staff, the appointment of senior palace staff is done by the king personally, other palace staff is appointed by senior palace personnel such as Secretary General of the Royal Court, provided that the appointee is certified for good conduct.

f) The right to pardon: Article 38 of the Jordanian Constitution states that the king has the right to pardon and to commute a sentence, as for general amnesty, a general amnesty is carried out by a special law. A pardon is in effect the punishment lifting of a sentenced person or group of people, either lifting it completely or partially without eliminating the consequences of the punishment or deleting the records, and is considered one of the king's rights as head of the executive branch. General amnesty on the other hand does not concern an individual or a group of individuals, but it targets a certain kind of crime or crimes that have occurred in certain circumstances. A general amnesty lifts the punishment and drops the charges and all consequences relating to it, and if a sentence has not been issued, stops the execution and procedures of the trial[1].
By examining Article 38 concerning the right of amnesty and pardon, we find that the right to pardon is given to the king, and that the right to issue general amnesty is in the hands of the legislature (Legislative branch) since it requires the issuance of a special law[2].

g) The right to declare war, conclude peace, and make treaties:
The King in the Jordanian political system is the head of state and head of the executive branch, that is in charge of defending and ensuring the security and safety of kingdom, and therefore the king has been given the right to declare war by the constitution. The king exercises that right through the cabinet since the cabinet is liable before the house of representatives. The process of peace treaties and pacts is also one

---

[1] Adel, Hiyari, **IBID,** P.690.

[2] Article 38 of the Jordanian Constitution and Article 39, stating that no death sentence shall be executed unless ratified by the king, and every such verdict is presented to the king with an appeal and an opinion from the Council of Ministers, Dr. Hiyari sees that such situations also needs a royal decree signed by the council of ministers since pardons also requires the signature of the Prime Minister and the ministers concerned.

of the king's rights, yet, no explicit legal provisions exist requiring the king to obtain approval from parliament in the case of a peace pact[1]. In relation to the issue of conventions and treaties, the second paragraph of article 33 states that if a treaty or convention results in expenses to the treasury or if such conventions or treaties alter public or personal rights of Jordanians. they shall not be valid unless approved by the National Assembly, and in no event shall the secret conditions of the treaty or agreement contradict the public terms of that treaty or convention.

h) Rights of the king as head of the royal family:

The king is considered head of the royal family, and has the right to monitor the royal family and the actions of its members, titles such as prince or princess are granted by the king to members of the royal family, and the king has the right to deprive any person of such title, The king also approves the royal family's weddings and divorces, the king also has the right to monitor the spending of the royal family from the money allocated to them from the budget, as the king may cancel these allocations or any portion thereof at any time, all aforementioned rights are personal rights of His Majesty the King carried directly and with no other person's involvement. [2]

i) the king's right to ratification of laws:

Article (31) of the Constitution states that "The King ratifies the laws and promulgates them. He shall direct the enactment of such regulations as may be necessary for their implementation, provided that such regulations are not inconsistent with the provisions thereof".

j) King's right in appointment of judicial council chairman and accepting his resignation accepting and appointment of constitutional court chairman and members and their resignation acceptance: Appointment of Army commander (Army General Head Quarters) and general intelligence director and police director genderma and the termination of their services. King's right in crown prince choosing and deputy king

---

[1] Article 33 of the Jordanian Constitution, paragraph (1), stipulates that "The King declares war and concludes peace and ratifies treaties and agreements" and this is the amendment of Article 33 publication number 1396 Date 01.09.1958 of the Official Gazette.

[2] Adel, Hiyari, **IBID**, P.P. 6680689. Article 116 of the Jordanian Constitution provides that "the king shall be paid from the General Revenue and appoint the general budget bill." For more information about the relationship between king authorities see Amin, Al-Mashaqba, (2012), **The King and the three powers**, Amman,: Dar Al-Hamid.

appointment by high royal will without prime ministers or minister in charge signature.

Council of Ministers:

Article (35) of the Jordanian Constitution states that: "The King appoints the Prime Minister and may dismiss him or accept his resignation. He appoints the Jordanian Ministers; he also dismisses them or accepts their resignation, upon the recommendation of the Prime Minister".

The council of ministers in the Hashemite Kingdom of Jordan is composed of the prime minister who is considered head of the council of ministers, and a number of ministers as needed and as required by the general interest of the country[1]. The Jordanian Constitution requires the that only Jordanians who do not hold a citizenship of any other country may be appointed ministers or equivalent[2], it is also not permissible for a working minister to be a member of the board of directors of any company or be involved in commercial or financial activity, or to receive a salary from any company, as well as to buy or rent any government property even if it is publicly auctioned[3]. A minister may be entrusted to one or more ministries as stated in the decree of appointment.

Before taking office, the Cabinet of ministers including the Prime Minister are sworn in before His Majesty the King, and the constitutional oath as stipulated in Article 43 of the Jordanian Constitution as "I swear by Almighty God to be loyal to the King, uphold the Constitution, serve the Nation and conscientiously perform the duties entrusted to me".

In general, the process of forming the ministry in the Hashemite Kingdom of Jordan is one of His Majesty the King's privileges. Relying on his constitutional right set out in Article 35 of the Jordanian Constitution, and it is the responsibility of the assigned prime minister to take into account in the formation of his ministry the competence and ability to achieve the endorsement of the house of representatives within a month of its formation, since the prime minister and the ministers are collectively responsible for the general policy in the Kingdom before the House of Representatives[4], the session of endorsement of the ministry or any minister of that ministry is called to by the prime minister or by at least ten members of the house of

---

[1]   Article 41 of the Jordanian Constitution.

[2]   Article 42 of the Jordanian Constitution.

[3]   Article 44 of the Jordanian Constitution.

[4]   Article 51 of the Jordanian Constitution.

representatives[1]. A ministry gains the endorsement is voted for by the absolute majority of the House of Representatives. This means that in the Jordanian political system, it is possible that the endorsement is not achieved. And in case the vote against the endorsement is made with an absolute majority of all members, the ministry must resign, and if the vote involved one minister, the minister must resign his post[2].

In the Jordanian political system, there is no restriction on being part of both the council of ministers or a prime minister and a part of the senate or House of Representatives at the same time, maintaining the right to vote, and the right to speak in both Houses.

As for the ministers who are not members of one of the houses they have the right to speak without the right to vote, as for ministers that are members of one of the houses, and that are paid as part of being ministers, such ministers are only compensated for their post as ministers and are not paid for being members of any of the houses, in other words it is not permissible for the minister to receive two salaries at the same time in case the minister is a member in the Senate or House of Representatives[3].

As for the process of appointing a member of the royal family as prime minister or a ministerial post, the Jordanian Constitution does not restrict the King in this regard, in other words, it is up to the king whether he wishes to designate a relative or any member of his family to form a cabinet or to entrust him to a ministry.

Secretary General of the Ministry:

Each of the ministries of Jordan has (Secretary General) a post formerly known as undersecretary of the Ministry, and it is known that secretary general of the ministry is a purely administrative post, where a secretary general of a ministry undertakes all administrative affairs of his ministry, and is also considered an assistant to the minister in the administration of the ministry, in the Jordanian political system, the secretary general's post is not affected by the formation or the resignation of a cabinet, meaning that he is not appointed when a cabinet is appointed, and is not dismissed when a cabinet is dissolved. As he is considered a public servant or a government employee, a secretary general of a ministry may substitute and act on behalf of the minister in attending

---

[1]   Article 54 of the Jordanian Constitution, the Ministry has to maintain the confidence of the House of Representatives during its period.

[2]   Article 53 of the Jordanian Constitution.

[3]   Article 52 of the Jordanian Constitution.

sessions of the legislative council and may speak on behalf of the minister on the affairs of the ministry to which he belongs[1]

The functions of the executive branch: Authority of Work System:

In Jordanian Statute, under Article 26 of the Constitution, the executive authority is given to the king, practiced through his minister. The king is immune from any liability or responsibility because the ministry is collectively responsible before the National Assembly for the public policy of the Kingdom, as for the terms of reference of the executive authority, part of that has been covered, specifically the part about the king's authority, In this part we will talk about the function of rules and regulations (sub legislation), where rules and regulations are issued by the executive authority for the purpose of clarifying and formalizing the details of the laws set by the legislative authority. As the legislative authority is the authorized body in creating laws, the rules and regulations set by the executive authority are made to facilitate the execution of such laws. Legislation is dominant over rules and regulations, as the rule or regulation is subject to legislation, and therefore cannot contradict any provisions of the legislation, and legislation can also cancel rules and regulations, the monitoring of the compliance of rules and regulations is a judiciary task and therefore carried out by the judiciary authority. The judiciary authority may cancel any rule or regulation that is not in line with the legislation in the kingdom, The Constitutional Court is the court that monitors the constitutionality of laws and regulations in force in the Kingdom. Regulations are divided into several types:

1) Executive regulation.
2) Independent regulation.
3) Legislative regulations.

1 - Executive regulations:

Defined as regulations issued to implement the laws passed by the legislative authority, Article 31 of the Constitution mentions this type or regulation by stating "The King ratifies the laws and promulgates them. He shall direct the enactment of such regulations as may be necessary for their implementation, provided that such regulations are not inconsistent with the provisions thereof".

---

[1] Article 52 of the Jordanian Constitution, this and that the appointment of the Secretary General of the ministry is done through a decision of the Council of Ministers and by a Royal Decree.

And executive regulations are one of the most important responsibilities of the executive branch, and since the carrying and enforcement of laws and legislation is the responsibility of the executive branch, the creation of regulations that allow such implementation is in line with the executive authority's purpose, yet regulations must not contradict with laws, for the existence of regulations is to implement laws provided they do not violate any provisions of the laws.

2 - Independent regulations

Such systems are not associated with any law and therefore are stand-alone systems, any independent system based on independent regulations exists to tackle certain matters without being based on laws issued by the legislative authority, and hence the naming, this type of regulation is divided into two types, public interest regulations, and control and disciplinary regulations.

A - Public interests regulations Regulations issued by the executive authority to regulate public utilities where it specifies how to establish such utilities and methods of organizing such utilities. This is based on constitutional provision 114 and provision 120 of the constitution, which lays down the basis for administrative divisions, and the establishment of government departments, and the recruitment of employees and their dismissal, and the supervision on government employees and managing their privileges, all the aforementioned are regulated through regulations issued by the council of ministers issued with the approval of the king. Such regulations may not extend to topics other than the aforementioned or they will be deemed unconstitutional.

B – Disciplinary regulations Regulations issued by the executive authority encompassing general rules and regulations meant to restrict individuals in order to maintain general order in society. General order is outlined by three main concepts, namely: security, tranquillity, and public health.

Terms of reference of the executive branch in a state of emergency:

In dangerous emergencies that threaten the security, safety and stability of any country, the executive branch is given extraordinary powers to deal with dangerous situations that may not be resolvable through existing normal laws.

In the Jordanian political system, like all other systems around the world, the constitution grants the executive branch additional, exceptional powers to remedy the exceptional dangerous circumstance affecting the kingdom, and in order to maintain public safety, security, and stability, and the rights given to the executive authority in these cases are the right to enforce the defense law, and the declaration of martial law in accordance to articles 124 and 125 of the Constitution.

3 - legislative regulations:

Legislation is the most important function of the legislature, yet the executive branch has been given the right to legislate in specific cases outlined by the constitution, especially in urgent matters and cases of emergency, matters that cannot be delayed. Yet this right was given to the executive authority provided certain conditions are held and met, conditions that may not be overlooked, rules and regulations issued and passed by the executive authority are called provisional (temporary) laws and are issued based on necessity. This is granted because the state establishes the law as the means and not the goal, and if an emergency should arise that requires the issuing of such laws, and the emergency fits a criteria of specific circumstances, then in such circumstances, the executive branch is given legislative authority as stipulated in article 94 of the constitution that reads.

1- In cases where the National Assembly House of Representatives or is dissolved, the Council of Ministers has, with the approval of the King, the power to issue provisional laws. Such laws are made to counter situations such as:

a) General disaster.
b) War and emergency situations.
c) The need for necessary and urgent funding that cannot be delayed.

Such provisional (temporary) laws are enforced in the same way other laws are enforced, provisional (temporary) laws can not violate the constitution, and such laws must be presented to the national assembly on the first session succeeding the issuance of the law, and the national assembly must reach a verdict on those laws within two normal consecutive sessions from the date they are submitted, and it is up to the national assembly on whether such laws are passed or rejected, if a provisional (temporary) law is rejected, or the period mentioned in this paragraph has passed without the approval or rejection of the law, the law is considered invalid and the council of ministers must obtain the approval of the king and then declare that law as invalid effective immediately, and from the date of the declaration, the law shall cease to have the force of law as long as it does not affect contracts and acquired rights.

2- Provisional laws shall have the same force and effect as laws enacted in accordance with paragraph (ii) of Article (93) of this Constitution.

Terms of reference of the Council of Ministers:

The first paragraph of article 45 of the Jordanian constitution makes a statement on the Terms of reference of the Council of Ministers as follows: "The Council of Ministers shall be entrusted with the responsibility of administering all affairs of the State, internal and external, with the exception of such matters as are or may be entrusted by the present Constitution or by any other legislation law to any other person or body".

This text is a general one, where the specifics and the details are dealt with through rules and regulations set forth by the Council of Ministers and are approved by the King to govern the workings of the executive authority, and the aforementioned is what the second paragraph of this Article (45) states in this regard, and the fact is that the Council of Ministers draws its competence through the reality of the executive function, as the implementation of laws is of the core of the Council's responsibility, and looking at the definition of government stating that it is the higher executive and administrative body in a state that carries the enforcement of laws and regulations in addition to all administrative tasks in public institutions, meaning that the government resembles the General mandate, and those competencies can be summarized as follows[1]:

1. Undertake the work of the higher management of the state and all public institutions.
2. Forming and implementing the public policy of the state in both internal and external affairs, and to exercise all functions and competencies to achieve that.
3. To oversee and supervise all governmental function in the light of the general policy.
4. To function as the King's Council and to take responsibility for the King in front of the National Assembly.
5. The management of public facilities and utilities base on the Constitution and the laws and regulations in force in the Kingdom.
6. Implementing the Constitution, legislation and regulations, as well as international treaties and conventions, regional and bilateral treaties and any other contracts committed to by the government.
7. To propose draft laws and regulations in all matters relating to public interest.
8. To appoint and dismiss staff in accordance with regulations.

---

[1]   Adel, Heyari, **IBID**, Andre, Horiu, (1977), **Constitutional law and political institutions**, P.418. Amin, Al-Mashaqbeh, (2006), **National Education,** P.204.

9. Preparing the general budget of the state.
10. Management of the state's economic affairs, and the organization of development projects and plans to develop the national economy.

The Council of Ministers exercises its rights and powers without the approval of the National Assembly unless stated by law. Article 48 of the Constitution states that: "His Prime Minister and Ministers shall sign the decisions taken by the Council of Ministers, which shall be submitted to the King for ratification in all cases required under the present Constitution or any law or regulations enacted thereunder. Such decisions shall be implemented by the Prime Minister and Ministers, each within the limits of his competence", and a minister is responsible for the administration of all matters pertaining to his ministry, and must submit any matter that is outside his terms of reference to the Prime Minister where the Prime Minister acts within his competence and submits whatever is beyond that to the Council of Ministers to take the necessary decisions.

Ministerial responsibility:

Ministerial responsibility is considered one of the most important elements of the parliamentary system, and what is meant by Ministerial responsibility of a minister or the ministry is what relates to the public interest, responsibility can be a collective responsibility where the entire ministry is liable, or individual responsibility where a minister is liable, and responsibility has various classifications, including political responsibility, punished by resignation or the non-endorsement of the ministry where it then must give up power, as for the civil responsibility of ministers, what it means is that a minister is responsible for compensating for damages resulting from their actions, while criminal responsibility is dealt with through the courts of law, where a minister is trailed for crimes punishable by law, as for the responsibility of ministers in the Hashemite Kingdom of Jordan, article 51 of the Constitution stipulates that "The Prime Minister and Ministers shall be collectively jointly responsible before the Chamber of Deputies in respect of the public policy of the State. In addition, each Minister shall be responsible before the Chamber of Deputies in respect of the affairs of his Ministry".

The session for vote of no confidence in the council of Ministers or in any Minister shall be held either at the request of prime Minister or at the request signed by a number of not less than ten members of the house of Representative. The vote of confidence shall be postponed for one time not exceed ten days and the house shall not be dissolved during this period.

Every formed council of Ministers shall place its ministerial statement to the house within one month of the date of its formation and shall obtain the vote of confidence by absolute

majority, if the house voted no confidence the council of ministers should resign.

Minister trials:

Legal proceedings concerning ministers over crimes resulting from their position as ministers are carried out before the regular courts competent in the capital, Amman, The house of representatives has been given the rights to submit ministers to the Attorney General along with reasons justifying such submission, every minister accused by the public prosecutor is suspended from work, this and that a minister's resignation does not stop the proceedings against him[1].

The resignation of the Cabinet:

There is a difference between the resignation of the Cabinet and a cabinet reshuffle, a cabinet reshuffle is when ministers are replaced by other ministers while maintaining the same prime minister, while resigning a ministry or cabinet means the formation of a generally different cabinet, it is permissible for the resigned prime minister to be appointed to form the new ministry, unless there has been a dissolution of the house of representatives during that prime minister's term, in such a case, that prime minister may not be appointed during the very next ministry, as Article (50) of the Constitution states that a resignation of the Prime Minister, his dismissal or death, all minister's in his cabinet are subject to dismissal. The dismissal of a ministry is a right given to the king as part of being the head of the executive branch based upon article 35 of the constitution.

Legislative authority in Jordan

This section deals with the legislative authority in the Jordanian political system in terms of its composition and terms of reference. As the legislative power is delegated to the National Assembly and the King, where the National Assembly consists of the Senate and a house of representatives[2].

---

[1]   Articles 55, 56 and 57 of the Jordanian Constitution.

[2]   Article 25 of the Jordanian Constitution.

A - **The Senate:**

In the Jordanian political system, members of the senate are appointed by the King, where Article 36 of the Jordanian Constitution stipulates that "The King appoints members of the Senate and appoints the Speaker from amongst them and accepts their resignation.", the King is also entitled to dissolve the senate or dismiss a member of the senate, appointment is done through a royal decree issued in this regard, the royal decree here is signed by the prime minister and the minister of interior[1]. As for the number of members of the Senate, article 63 of the Jordanian Constitution specifies that number as follows "The Senate, including the Speaker, shall consist of not more than one- half of the number of the members of the Chamber of Deputies", and according to the electoral law of 2016, the senate consists of 65 members including the head of the senate, and that is half of the 130 which is the number of members in the house of representatives.

Article 64 of the Jordanian Constitution defines eligibility for senate membership as follows[2]:

1) Must have completed forty calendar years of age.
2) Must belong to one of the following classes.

A. Present and former Prime Ministers and Ministers.
B. Has previously served in one of the following positions:

1) Previously held the office of Ambassador.
2) Speaker of the Chamber of Deputies.
3) President and judges of the Court of Cassation and of the Civil and Sharia Courts of Appeal.
4) Retired military officers of the rank of Lt. General and above.
5) Former Deputies who were elected at least twice as deputies
6) Other similar personalities who enjoy the confidence of the people in view of the services rendered by them to the Nation and the Country. As for Article 75 of the Jordanian Constitution, enumerating the

---

[1] In addition to the right of the king to appoint members of the Senate, and after the amendment to article 34 published in issue 2533 Date 10.11.1974 of the Official Gazette in addition to the latter part of the fourth paragraph it "the king may dissolve the Senate or dismiss one of its members."

[2] Article 64 of the Jordanian Constitution. Article 75 of the Jordanian Constitution as contained in the text, stipulate the conditions of membership that apply to both chambers (Senators and Representatives)

conditions that prohibit an individual from being part of the senate or the House of Representatives, the article reads no person shall become a Senator or Deputy:

(a) Who is not a Jordanian.
(b) Who claims foreign nationality or protection.
(c) Who was adjudged bankrupt and has not been legally discharged.
(d) Who was interdicted and the interdiction has not been removed.
(e) Who was sentenced to a term of imprisonment exceeding one year for a non- political offence and has not been pardoned.
(f) Who is insane or an imbecile.
(g) Who is related to the King within a degree of consanguinity to be prescribed by special law.

The second paragraph of this same article stipulates that people who meet following criteria do not qualify as members of the senate, the criteria states that "he who has a material interest in any contract, other than a lease of land and property, with any Department of Government, provided that this provision shall not apply to any shareholder in a company of more than ten members "is ineligible to become a senator".

Members meeting any ineligibility criterion, or where paragraph two applies, membership of the senate or House of Representatives is revoked automatically. The Jordanian constitution stipulates that the membership term for the senate is four years, where new members of the senate are appointed Every four years, and it is permissible to reappoint members with expired memberships, the term for the head of the senate is two years, head of senate may be reappointed upon expiry of his term[1].

In case of a vacancy in the senate whether due to a member's decease or a resignation or for any other reason, the vacancy is filled by appointment, the appointment must be carried within two months of the assembly's notification to the government, the term of membership for the substitute member lasts until the expiry of his predecessor's term[2]. As for the senate's sessions, The senate is in session whenever the house of representatives is in sessions, as sessions are shared among both houses, and if the dissolution of the House of Representatives should occur, sessions of the Senate are also ceased[3].

---

[1]   Article 65 paragraph (1) or paragraph (2)

[2]   Article 88 of the Jordanian Constitution.

[3]   Article 66 of the Jordanian Constitution.

B - The House of Representatives:

Jordanian parliament consists of two chambers: the Senate and the House of Representatives, and based on Article 67 of the Constitution, the House of Representatives consists of the elected members elected in a general, secret and direct manner, according to the election law, which guarantees the following principles:

A. Integrity of the election.
B. candidates have the right to monitor the electoral process.
C. Punishment of those who attempt to undermine the will of the voters.

As for the generic nature of the election, Jordanian elections are not absolutely general as some groups of people are not eligible for voting, those restrictions are the prerequisites of an eligible voter which in itself does not contradict the principle of a general election, as the right to vote stays general for those who have completed 18 years of age provided he or she is registered to vote, based on the electoral law number 28 of 2012.

What is meant by secret is that a voter does not need to declare who he or she has voted for, and the purpose of that is so that the results in the ballot are representative of the joint will of the voters, as an explicit and no secret election could have certain drawbacks such as being affected by the surroundings which in turn will affect the integrity of the result, as for the meaning of a direct election, it means that a voter votes directly for who he or she wants, and not through a delegate or a representative, the exception to that are illiterates who cannot write, in that case, the vote is carried out by whispering to the ear of the head of the committee[1].

Term of the House of Representatives:

The House of Representatives' term is four calendar years, starting from the date of announcement of the results of the general election in the Official Gazette, and the king may extend the term to a period of not less than one year and not more than two years.

Independent Election Commission:

The Constitution states in the second paragraph of Article 67 that an independent commission that oversees the election and administers it at all

---

[1]   The Jordanian Election law No. 28 of 2012.

stages must be established, this commission also oversees any other election the council of ministers decides to hold, the law of the commission has been issued as No. 11 of 2012 dated 09/04/2012.

Jordanian Election law:

The amended election law was issued as number 6 for the year 2016, on May,22,2016, this law defined an eligible voter as any Jordanian who is or will be over 18 calendar years of age on the date of the vote, such voter has the right to vote for a representative according to this law. This right is suspended and not in effect for members and staff of the Jordanian Arab army, and the Jordanian intelligence department, public security, gendarmerie and civil defence while in active service, also ineligible for the vote are:

1) Who was adjudged bankrupt and has not been legally discharged.
2) Who is insane or an imbecile or interdicted.

The department of Civil Status does not issue election cards to those who are ineligible to vote.

The Independent Commission for the election requires that the Department of Civil Status issues election cards according to a set of standards issued through executive regulations set for this particular purpose. Election cards are made for every eligible voter who has a personal ID card with a national number printed on that card, according to the place of residence, and according to the electoral constituencies. The voting card is handed to the voter himself, or to any other person specified by the executive regulations in this matter, after which the department of civil status creates tables and lists of voters for every constituency, and hands them to the independent elections commission, where the commission publishes those tables along with relevant objections on their website, or in any media they deem appropriate for this purpose. Voters are allowed to object in addition to appeals, and after considering objections and appeals, the tables and lists are considered final and the election for the house of representatives will then be held according to those tables.

According to the law of 2016, The kingdom is divided into a number of local constituencies, allocated allocates fifteen (15) parliamentary seats for women (women's quota), and that this does not exclude Bedouins and the aforementioned quotas stipulated by this law.

According to the law, the number of members of the House of Representatives is 130 members, and the law which relied on open-list method, the list should include aminimum of 3 candidates, and more than the number of seats assigned to the constituency voters cast their votes on one list and then votes on one list and then vote for each candidate on the list.

The kingdom was divided into 23 electoral districts or constituencies, including three Bedouin constituencies and one general electorate (constituency) in the Kingdom. The law specifies the conditions that must apply for the candidate to run the election as follows:

1. Jordanian since at least ten years.
2. Does not carry the nationality of another State.
3. To have completed thirty calendar years of age on polling day.
4. Has not been adjudged bankrupt without been legally discharged.
5. Who was interdicted and the interdiction has not been removed.
6. Must not have been sentenced to a term of imprisonmen exceeding one year for a non-political offense and has not been pardoned.
7. Who is insane or an imbecile.
8. Who is related to the King within a degree of consanguinity to be prescribed by special law.
9. should not be contracted with any official governmental public institutions or public companies or any official institution neither directly or indirectly, exceptions are a land and property lease, Also exempt is a shareholder in a company among at least ten other partners, the law also stipulates that it is not permissible for ministers, employees of ministries, employees of governmental departments, employees of governmental organizations or official bodies, employees of official Arab and international bodies and institutions, the head of the municipality, heads of city municipal councils, members of city municipal councils, and municipality employees to run for the election unless they resign their position at least two months prior to the candidate registration date, and whoever wishes to register as a candidate for the house of representatives must first be registered as a voter, and must pay a non-refundable JD500 to the treasury, a candidate may only run for the election in one constituency.

Sessions of the National Assembly:

In the Jordanian political system there are three types of sessions of the National Assembly, and what is meant by a session is the duration of the meeting which is being held between the members of the national assembly, the types of sessions are:

1. Ordinary sessions.

2. Extraordinary sessions.
3. Special sessions.

1) Ordinary Sessions:

Based on the Jordanian Constitution, the National Assembly is to hold one ordinary session on every year of the house's term[1]. The constitution specifies the length of the ordinary session to be 6 months unless the king dissolves the House of Representatives before the end of the period.

2) Extraordinary sessions:

In the case where the house of representatives is dissolved, and after a general election, the new House of Representatives meet in an extraordinary session, and this session is subject to the terms of the constitution where the terms relating to extension and delay will apply.

3) Special sessions:

There are two methods to call for a special sessions of the National Assembly of Jordan, the first method is when the king of Jordan solely calls for a special session, as stated in article 82 of the constitution where it reads "The king may call for a special session for an indefinite duration when needed for the purpose of ratification of certain matters that are stated in the royal decree" The second method: The king calls for a session based upon the request of the House of Representatives.

Parliamentary immunity:

The Jordanian Constitution gave certain immunities to members of the National Assembly of Jordan, both Senate and House of Representatives in order to conduct matters related to the public interest within the council, freely and without fear or influence of the executive branch or any other, This immunity means that no member of the national assembly may be charged or held on charge during the duration of the council meeting unless the house of which that person is a member decides and agrees to do so, and that member may not be charged or held on basis of a charge unless he or she was caught red handed in a criminal offense.

---

[1] Article 8 of the amended election law No. 6 for the year 2016. See the text of Article 77 of the Jordanian Constitution.

The dissolution of the House of Representatives:

What dissolution of the House of Representatives means is to end the term of the house before the term specified by the constitution expires, and according to the constitution, the power to dissolve the House of Representatives was given to the executive branch represented by the king[1].

The King undertakes the dissolution of the house of representatives through a royal decree, this royal decree is signed by the prime minister and the relevant minister, and the executive branch's ability to dissolve the house of representatives is based on the fact that the house of representatives can revoke the endorsement of the government or not endorse the government at all. And therefore the executive branch was given the right to dissolve the House of Representatives provided a reason for the dissolution is given.

The constitutional amendment of 2011 stipulates that the government which the house of representatives is dissolved during its term is to resign within a week of the date of dissolution, and the prime minister of that government may not be reappointed on the very next formation. This amendment creates an imbalance in terms of the balance between the executive and the legislative branch, and is a new restriction imposed on the powers of the king.

The functions of the legislative authority

In the Jordanian political system, the legislative authority plays a key role within its constitutional competence of proposing laws and approving them, and monitors the executive branch in all circumstances, whether normal or exceptional. This monitoring is called the political competence or the political supervision of the legislative branch, in addition the legislator has a financial competence, as there can be "no tax without a law", and the general budget of the country is not issued unless approved through a law by the legislator, and as can be clearly seen from the constitution, there are three main competencies and functions of the legislator in Jordan which are:

1. The legislative competence.
2. The political competence (supervision).
3. The financial competence.

---

[1] Article 34 of the Jordanian Constitution stated that the constitutional period of the House of Representatives is four years where any termination of the term of the House of Representatives by the executive branch before the end of that period is considered dissolution.

Legislative competence:

The normal process of legislation goes through a number of stages, starting with the proposal of a law, followed by the approval of the law, then the ratification and publishing.

A - The proposal stage:

Since the legislative authority is the competence of the National Assembly and the King, the process of proposing laws is the competence of the legislator (National Assembly), and the executive branch (council of ministers). The executive branch in the kingdom has the right to propose new laws, where article 91 of the constitution states: "The Prime Minister shall refer to the Chamber of Deputies any draft law, and the Chamber shall be entitled to accept, amend, or reject the draft law".

As for the right of the legislator to propose laws, the first paragraph of article 95 of the constitution states that: "Any ten or more Senators or Deputies may propose any law. Such proposal shall be referred to the committee concerned in the House for its views. If the House is of the opinion that the proposal be accepted it shall refer it to the Government for drafting it in the form of draft law, and to submit it to the House either during the same session or at the following session".

B - Approval (of laws) stage:

Article "91" of the Constitution clarifies that the approval of laws is the competence of the national assembly (senate and representatives) where it reads "No law may be promulgated unless approved by both houses and ratified by the King."

C - The law ratification stage:

Ratification of laws is a key element in the process of legislation. Ratification is the approval of the Head of State (King) upon the approval of a law by the legislature. As based on the provisions contained in the Jordanian Constitution, the "King ratifies the law" and that "no law may be promulgated unless passed by both houses and ratified by the King[1]". The Jordanian Constitution also sets the method of ratification, where Article (93) of the Constitution states in paragraph (1) that: "Every draft law passed by the Senate and the Chamber

---

[1]   Article 31, and Article 91 of the Jordanian Constitution.

of Deputies shall be submitted to the King for ratification." and the second paragraph stipulates that "If the King does not see fit to ratify a law, He may, within six months from the date on which the law was submitted to him, refer it back to the House coupled with a statement showing the reasons for withholding his ratification."

D - The law issuance and publication stage:

A law is published and declared after being approved by the legislator and after passing the aforementioned stages. The king is in charge of issuing laws, and delegates to the executive branch the task putting a law into force, and overseeing its implementation. Article (31) of the Constitution states that "The King ratifies the laws and promulgates them. He shall direct the enactment of such regulations as may be necessary for their implementation, provided that such regulations are not inconsistent with the provisions thereof. "while the second paragraph of Article (93) of the Constitution, stipulates that "A law shall come into force after its promulgation by the King and the lapse of thirty days from the date of its publication in the Official Gazette unless it is specifically provided in that law that it shall come into force on any other date."

Political competence of the legislator:

What is meant by the political competence of the legislator (the Jordanian national assembly) is the supervision carried out by the national assembly over the executive branch, those supervisory actions are namely:

1 - Questioning

Questioning is a member's inquiry on a matter he or she does not know or a desire to verify an event that he has been informed of, as well as inquiring about the government's intention on a certain matter.

2 - Interrogation:

Interrogation is defined as "Holding Minister accountable for behavior or actions taken in a public affair[1]". I other words, requesting the council of ministers or a minister to provide information or data on any matter relating to public policy, interrogation is considered of a higher level than the question

---

[1] Article 94 of the Rules of Procedure of the House of Representatives.

since it is considered an act of holding the ministry or a minister accountable for a certain matter. The right to interrogation is given to the members of Senate and Chamber of Deputies as a constitutional right, as stipulated in Article (96) of the Constitution.

3 - Investigation:

The national assembly has the right to investigate for the purpose of seeking knowledge or verifying certain matters, and the assembly has the right to contact governmental institutions and the right to examine files relating to that specific matter. Investigation is carried through special committees formed for this purpose, the committee or committees submit their findings to the house relying on those findings for decision making in the matter being investigated.

4 - Display of interest:

Based on the principle of ministerial responsibility, and the right of the national assembly to monitor and supervise the executive branch, members of the national assembly whether Senate and Deputies may express their interest or make specific proposals to the executive to undertake. Provided that such proposals are in the public interest and aim to serve the community as a whole.

5 - Listen to petitions:

It is the right of Jordanian citizens to submit petitions to the authorities in the kingdom, as well as to submit petitions to the national assembly.

Terms of reference Specific to the House of Representatives:

Even though the principle in effect is the principle of equality between the houses, there are matters that are the competence of the House of Representatives alone, namely.

1. A vote for endorsement of the ministry or any Minister. Article (53) of the Constitution.
2. Accusing ministers and referring them to Public Prosecution, Article (56) of the Constitution.
3. An absolute majority of deputies may call for a special session for the national assembly. Article (82) of the Constitution.
4. The Audit Bureau as a supervising body is tied to the National Assembly, Article (119) of the Constitution.

Financial competence of the National Assembly:

Chapter VII of the Constitution is dedicated to financial affairs. The role of the national assembly is in this regard comes through constitutional provisions contained, for no tax or fee may be imposed without a law. All taxes, fees and any other funds the government collects are considered part of the state treasury, while various costs and expenses are set through a law.

Article (117) of the Jordanian Constitution provides that "Any concession granting a right for the exploitation of mines, minerals or public utilities shall be sanctioned by law."

What is meant by the general state budget is "the financial document" that is determined by the income and expenditure of the state. This document is a balance and demonstrates the relationship between income and expenditure, where income and expenditure are put into one perspective and tailored in order to achieve certain goals and objectives at a future stage.

State budgeting is technically considered administrative work, yet theoretically, it is considered a law and a legal matter because in order to set the budget, a law is required, and that law is issued by the legislative authority.

The process of adopting a budget plan:

The Jordanian Constitution sets the rules to be taken into account while approving a draft budget law:

A. Voting on the budget chapter by chapter.
B. The right to reduce expenditures without increasing them.
C. No existing tax may be cancelled or impose or modify.
D. Expenses or incomes bound by valid contracts may not be modified.
E. general budgets are set annually.

Audit Bureau:

Article (119) of the Jordanian Constitution declares that an Audit Bureau must be formed in order to monitor income and expenditure of the state and disbursement methods. And according to the law, a higher authority called the audit bureau is established to monitor and supervise financial affairs, working under the authority of the House of Representatives, and working on behalf of the house of representatives in monitoring and supervising ministries, public utility, municipalities, public governmental institutions, and any form of special public bodies[1].

Judiciary authority

The judiciary is an authority independent of all other authorities, this authority is handled by various courts and issues it's verdicts in accordance with the laws of the kingdom. Article (27) of the Jordanian Constitution, states: "The Judicial Power shall be exercised by the courts of law in their varying types and degrees. All judgments shall be given in accordance with the law and pronounced in the name of the King".

Courts in the Kingdom are open to all and shall be free and protected from any interference in their affairs, which means that everyone is entitled to seek justice through the courts and there can be no interference in the judicial authority's work whether from an official or unofficial party.

In addition to the principle of judiciary independence in the Jordanian judicial system and the principle of equality before the courts, the Jordan judicial system adopts one more principle that is the free judiciary services, what this principle implies is that the judiciary services are provided for free, and that no fee is imposed on litigation services. And that all members of the judiciary receive their salaries from the state, while litigation is free, paying fees for certain expenses is not inconsistent with the principle of free judiciary services in the Hashemite Kingdom of Jordan. As the judiciary service is considered a public service meant to protect the public interest and preserve the rights of others, public hearings is also a principle taken by the judiciary system in Jordan regarded as one of the fundamental guarantees of litigation integrity, in addition to promoting confidence among litigants[2].

To ensure proper administration of justice, the Jordanian judiciary system has taken the principle litigation on two stages, allowing the loosing litigant to seek litigation at the second level of litigation for a higher verdict, promoting confidence in justice, and the ability to submit the dispute to a higher court also promotes better practice at the Courts of First Instance, Courts of First

---

[1] to the terms of reference of the legislature Amin Al-Mashaqbeh, (2005), **National Education and the Jordanian political system**, Edition 7, PP.195-215.

[2] In some cases public hearings can have a negative effect on the litigants and the public, in such cases it is possible that hearings become confidential if the Court finds that appropriate in order to take into account public order or to avoid a public nuisance and as stipulated in Article 101, paragraph (2) of the Jordan Constitution, stating that "The sittings of the courts shall be public unless the court considers that it should sit in camera in the interest of public order or morals"

Instance look into claims and charges submitted for the first time, courts of higher instance look into charges submitted for the second time, namely, Second instance courts are formally called the Courts of Appeal. And on top of the judicial system hierarchy is the Courts of cassation, ensuring the proper application and interpretation of the law. The principle of two stage judicial system is one of the important principles that guarantee the integrity of the judicial system.

Judges in the Jordanian political system are independent, restricted only by law, appointment of judges in Jordanian courts, promotion, or dismissal is done through a decision of the judicial Council combined with a royal decree in accordance with the provisions of the law[1].

Judge or judges include the following positions: Head of the Court of Cassation, President and members of the Supreme Court of Justice, Chief Public Prosecutor, Assistant to the Secretary-General of the Ministry of Justice, legislation judges, justice inspector, and members of the Courts of Appeal, the Attorney General and his aides, and members of the Courts of First Instance, judges of municipality of the capital, members of municipal courts, magistrates, prosecutors, and any judge whose appointment is the competence of the Jordanian judicial Council[2].

Types of courts in Jordan:

Based on article "99" of the Jordanian Constitution, there are three types of courts:

1. civil courts.
2. Religious courts.
3. special Courts.

1 - Civil courts:

The Act which civil courts are formed was issued under No. 26 of 1952, and has been amended more than once in order to accommodate changes relating to the kingdom where the last amendment to this Law was No. 31 for the year 2008, published in the Official Gazette issue No. 4910 Date 1/6 / 2008 (amended law for the formation of the regular courts) (3). This is the law that regulates the formation of regular courts in the Kingdom and identifies their

---

[1]   Article 98 of the Jordanian Constitution.

[2]   Adib, Alhlsa, (1971), **foundations of legislation and the judicial system in the Jordan**, Cairo: Institute of Research and Arab Studies, P.85.

competence at various levels and kinds. Regular courts in the Kingdom are categorized into several types, namely:

1- the first level (magistrates' courts and courts of first instance).
2- The second level (the courts of appeal of which at the top of the hierarchy is the Court of Cassation, which is considered among the courts of appeal and is not considered a third level court.

All aforementioned courts have competencies in civil, commercial and criminal cases, added to that there is administrative litigation which is the competence of the Supreme Court of Justice.

A - Magistrates Courts:

Based on Article 3 of the law on the formation of civil courts No. 26 for the year 1952, magistrates' courts are formed in every district and village or anywhere else with a regulation set by the Council of Ministers with the consent of His Majesty the King. Such Courts are composed of a single judge named magistrate. The magistrates' courts considers criminal cases that are minor offenses and offenses punishable by imprisonment for a period not exceeding two years, along with crimes of perjury, and perjury arising in conciliation.

B- Courts of First Instance:

Based on the law on the formation of the regular courts in the Kingdom of Jordan, the formation of Courts of First Instance is done via a regulation issued by the Council of Ministers with the consent of His Majesty the King. The Courts of First Instance consist of a president and a number of judges as needed, such courts have competence over all civil and criminal cases except those exempted by special provisions (1).

Courts of First Instance function at two levels, the first as Courts of First Instance, with terms of reference covering civil cases, litigation concerning immovable property which is beyond the competence of magistrates' courts, as well as all criminal cases that fall outside the scope of the Magistrates Courts, Courts of First Instance also function as second level jurisdiction, where in some cases Magistrate's Court cases are appealed in Courts of First Instance provided the law stipulates that such a case is appealed through Courts of First Instance. Court of First Instance also considers appeals in any verdict set to be appealed in Court of First Instance, and when the court looks into charges punished by the death penalty, or by life imprisonment with hard labor, a committee of three judges is formed1 While a committee is composed of two judges in cases where other criminal charges are considered, and a single judge when considering offenses.

Juvenile Court:

Juvenile Court is the Magistrate's Court or the Court of First Instance sitting as Juvenile Court, based on Article five of the Juvenile Act No. 35 of 2007, a court looking into charges to a minor is considered a juvenile court.

Higher Criminal Court:

The higher criminal court was formed based on Law No. 33 of 1976, and is held with the head of the court holding a government ranking of at least second rank, and two with a government ranking no less than third in the judiciary system.

Judges and prosecutors of this court are bound by the same laws and regulations that apply to regular judges. This court is concerned with certain crimes taking place anywhere in the kingdom, crimes such as murder, rape, sexual assault, criminal kidnap, and the attempt of such crimes.

C - Courts of Appeal:

Based on paragraph A of article "6" of the provisional (temporary) law No. 12 of 1989 (Amended law on the Formation of Regular Courts)2. Courts of appeal are formed in Amman, Irbid, Ma'an, where a head of the court is appointed and a number of judges, the court can hold hearings in any location within its regional judicial authority with the consent of the minister of justice, and the work of the courts of appeal is the appeal of any charge or the reconsideration of verdicts reached by the courts of [1] first instance, since courts of appeal are higher in degree than courts of first instance. Courts of appeal do not have the right to look into any charge against any defendant or into any dispute if such a charge or dispute has not been submitted to the courts of first instance[2].

---

[1] Mohamed, Najem P.82. Farouk, Al-Kilani, (1966), **Special Courts in Jordan,** Edition1, Beirut, P.483. 2 Muhammad, Najm, **IBID,** P.83. Mufleh, Al Kthah, PP.65-66.

[2] Official Gazette on March 9, 1989 Issue 3614.

D - The Court of Cassation:

Based on Article nine of the amended Act of establishing regular courts No. 12 of 1989, paragraph (1).

1) The Court of Cassation is formed in Amman of a president and a number of judges, and is held with five judges in its regular session, headed by the senior Judge, in cases where an appeals court insists on a mismatching verdict, or if the charges in question revolve around a case resulting in new legal principal, or if the case is complex in certain aspects, or is of public significance, or if a certain committee sees to withdraw a principal set in a previous ruling, a committee formed from the president of the cassation court and eight judges is formed.

2) If the president of the cassation court does not participate in the committee's session, the senior judge becomes head of the committee, and an additional judge is called upon to complete the session quorum.

3) In case of different opinions, the Court issues its decision by majority vote.

As for the terms of reference of the Court of Cassation, the court looks into cases and verdicts from the court of appeals in criminal charges, and cases of no-trial issued by the public prosecutor in criminal cases.

And in its civil capacity when looking into civil charges and verdicts in civil cases handled by the court of appeals.

Administrative Legislation:

Administrative legislation no. (27) For the year 2014 was issued with a text in their third article calling to establish in the kingdom a legislation called Administrative legislation comprising:

A. The administrative court.
B. The high administrative court

Located in Amman and formed of a chairman and a number of members with not less than second degree. It is the legal successor of the high justice court. The administrative court is specialized in looking into all appeals related to final administrative decisions.

The administrative court specialization includes the following:

1. Municipal councils, commerce and industry chambers, associations and clubs registered in the kingdom election appeals, and the election

appeals that are conducted according to laws and systems in force and do not include procedures preceding voting process.

2. Appeals that are presented by whom they may concern in final administrative resolutions related to appointment in public posts and stopping annual increments to public employees.

3. Employees requests for cancelation of final administrative resolutions relating to termination with no legal channel.

4. Public employees requests for cancelation of final resolutions issued by against them by disciplinary boards.

5. Disputes related to retirement salaries due to retired public pensioners or their inheritors.

6. Legal suits presented by individuals or authorities for cancelation of final administrative resolutions.

7. Suits to malfunction any resolution made under a system violating constitution or law at request injured.

8. Claims and queries that are considered within high justice court scope of duties previously according to any other legislation.

Appeal relates to any resolution relating to any act of sovereignty is not accepted. The High Administrative Court in its two types is considered the highest legislative reference in Jordan concerning the scope of its duties as mentioned and its resolutions of high court are concluded and not subject to appeal or review. The appeal isn't acceptable by the two administrative courts in any decision related to sovereignty works.

As mentioned before the high administrative court is considered to be the highest legislative reference in Jordan in its field, and they are two administrative and systematical courts. The high court decisions are justified and not subject to appeal or review.

3 - Religious courts:

Based on Article 104 of the Jordanian Constitution, the religious courts are divided into two types: Sharia courts, and boards of other religious communities, where the later represents non-Muslim communities recognized by the Hashemite Kingdom of Jordan.

A - Sharia courts:

The law governing the formation of sharia courts issued on May 1st, 1951 requires the establishment sharia courts of first instance in district centres, or at any other location, that law also states that there must be one sharia appeal court or more as needed with regulations set by the Chief Justice in the Kingdom with the consent of His Majesty the King.

Sharia Courts of Appeal are composed of a president and a number of member judges and is known to go into session with a president and two judges, verdicts are issued with a majority vote and verdicts are final. Based on the law on the formation of the sharia courts, a sharia judicial council was formed and practices its competence in recommending and endorsing sharia judges for the purpose of appointment since the appointment of sharia judges is carried out through a royal decree.

As for the terms of reference of Sharia courts, article (105) of the Constitution stipulates "The Sharia Courts shall in accordance with their own laws have exclusive jurisdiction in respect of the following matters":

1) Matters of personal status of Moslems.
2) Cases concerning blood money (Diya) where the two parties are Moslems or where one of the parties is not a Moslem and the two parties consent to the jurisdiction of the Sharia Courts.
3) Matters pertaining to Islamic Waqfs.

B - Religious Community Councils:

Religious Community councils are councils formed to deal with matters of non-Muslim communities, communities recognized by the government as being established in the Hashemite kingdom of Jordan, Such councils are formed in accordance with the provisions of laws issued to address such councils, such laws outline the terms of reference for such councils relating to personal status affairs and the related endowments of those communities, personal status in the competence of such councils is the counterpart to the personal status affairs in Sharia courts in the case of Muslims. Examples of personal status affairs are marriage and all related inheritance, endowment of non-Muslim communities, will and testament, and all other matters concerning the community in the area of personal status. Every such community council recognized the Kingdom appoints a head of the council and a number of members, the council head and members must then be approved by the Council of Ministers and King[1].

---

[1] Article 108 and Article 109 of the Jordanian Constitution. Communities that have the right to establish councils in the Kingdom are the Greek Orthodox community, the Roman Catholic community, the Armenians, the roman orthodox community, and the Episcopal Anglican Communion, the Maronite community, the Lutheran Anglican Communion, The Syriac Orthodox, and Coptic Orthodox.

4 - **Special Courts:**

Based on Article 110 of the Constitution, special courts exercising jurisdiction in accordance with provisions of their own laws. Special courts carry this name because they consider certain matters and are not generic courts in nature. Special courts are linked to the Ministry of Justice, and are subject to all applicable laws and regulations. Judges of special courts are regular judges appointed by the Jordanian judicial council, and are bound to all laws and regulations of the judiciary. There are many special courts in the Kingdom, including the income tax Court of Appeal, the Court of state property, settlement court of real estate and water, the Customs Court both first instance and appellate, State security courts, Military tribunals, Administrative governor courts, Police courts and other special courts.

CHAPTER IV

Political Reform and Democracy

First topic Introduction:
Political reform :

SINCE 1989, THE Jordanian state has adopted the route of restoring democracy, broadening the level of democratic political participation, and therefore restoring life to the parliamentary and political party scene, legislation governing the establishment of such process came gradually, starting from the freezing of the martial law and cancelling it afterwards, followed by the issuance of law 32 of 1992, governing and allowing for political parties and a parliamentary election, in addition to the Press and publications law (10) for the year 1992 and the Defence Act No. 13 of 1992. Those laws formed a starting point for a new phase of development of the Jordanian state and its democratic system.

Generally, States refine their democratic system from time to time by learning from their experience, because of the changes in the surrounding variables that affect the system, leading to change in the laws and regulations that govern the democratic process to suit the higher national interest, especially security and safety, and to promote progress and development of the democratic system.

In addition to broadening participation and to create a satisfactory equitable representation of citizens, which drives up the regime's acceptance and legitimacy. The process of continuous revision of laws is based on the ongoing experience around the flaws of application, as part of these revisions, Jordan reviews, among other laws, the laws and regulations concerning the electoral and political party law, a priority due to its significance in supporting the democratic process and enforcing it, as well as allowing it to adapt to current political circumstance, electoral laws play an important role in pushing the democratic process forward, as in the law's essence are the fundamental principles of freedom, justice, equality, representation and participation, and to attain the aforementioned, democratic values and the widespread of democratic culture are needed, which in turn require awareness, education, a sense of belonging to the state, the establishment of the concept of citizenship, the demotion of smaller affiliations, the existence of a middle class which serves to enhance stability, the existence of active civil society organizations independent of political powers, add to that a good living standard, still a lot of these conditions have not yet been met, or are rather weak on the Jordanian political scene, taking into account that the Jordanian state is subject to the regional political circumstance, namely, the Arab-Israeli conflict and the failure to resolve this conflict is still a major influence on the political situation, in addition to the political instability of other Arab states in the light of the Arab spring, and its impact on the state of the affairs in the country, and in general political stability in the Middle East will be an important factor in the development and establishing of democracy in middle east countries. Needless to say, political reform requires the development of political and social educational system, side by side with the adaptation of political systems suitable for the surrounding changes, along with the advancement and development of the country's institutions of all kinds and types.

Jordanian National Charter:

In April 9, 1990, a royal decree was issued to establish the National Committee for the formulation of the National Charter, the committee was made of 60 members covering a spectrum of political, cultural, technical and professional members. The committee came out with the national charter which was made official in an official public conference on 9 June 1991.

The national charter is a political document setting the path for the political process, and aims to lay the foundations of national goals and determining subjects of importance, and to find General guidelines for political pluralism and democratic principles in order to build a democratic civil society[1].

The Charter is a political document that is not a substitute to the Constitution; rather, it aims to activate the constitution's principals and its values. taking into account circumstances that Jordan has been through, combined with resumed democratic life called to work on achieving a national consensus based on the minimum and common ground through serious national dialogue and a structure serving an intellectual and political framework to organize the relationship between governmental institutions and civil society at all levels.

The goal of the national Charter is to lay the basis of political and democratic work in a balance between rights and responsibilities, to build a balanced relationship between the institutions of government and society, to establish rules of justice and mutual respect, to promote institutionalization, to confirm constitutional, legal, and human rights to all Jordanians, to activate their role in decision-making through the establishment of democratic institutions, to broaden the base of political participation, and hence, the National Charter is a political agreement between all political forces and parties, laying down the path for general reform in all areas, political, social, educational, cultural, economical and finally political pluralism based upon the respect of the Jordanian state's political legitimacy, respect for the constitution, the participation of Jordanians of all backgrounds and classes in the political life, the building of democratic institutions, and the promotion of the sense of national belonging, which would enable to be a starting point and a new beginning towards a better future[2].

The national charter also lays down some constitutional axioms binding to all political forces and parties, such as: that the political system in the kingdom is a hereditary parliamentary monarchy, and the Jordanian people are part of the Arab nation, and the religion of the state is Islam, and that the Arabic language is the official language of the state, in addition to faith in God, the respect for spiritual values, and equality between all Jordanians, and their right to form political parties and organizations.

The national charter also contained values and principles regarding democracy, freedom, human rights, political pluralism, and the rule of law, such as: deepening the democratic approach, the finding of political pluralism, activating ideology and political parties, enabling public participation in governance through the establishment of democratic national institutions, the

---

[1] King Hussein Bin Talal's speech in his address to form the charter committee, Amman, April 1990.

[2] Ahmed, Obeidat, (1996), a lecture at the seminar of the National Charter, Amman, Royal Cultural Centre, June 1996.

adoption of democratic dialogue as the means to democracy, and to overcome terrorism, intolerance and violence.

The national charter defines the constitutional state as the state of all its citizens regardless of their ideologies, gaining its legitimacy from the free will of the people. Its strength is gained from the implementation of the principals of equality, justice, and equal opportunities.

The charter emphasized commitment to the principles of the rule of law and the respect for human rights, and to provide legal safeguards and judicial protection of those rights and to the preservation of human dignity. It also highlighted the adherence to the Jordanian constitution in both text and spirit in the state's journey, and in carrying out its executive, judicial and legislative functions. Tackling the principals of belonging and loyalty to the state the Charter is able to enforce the democratic approach that teaches the coming generations the values of sacrifice, faith in the homeland, and faith in the nation's causes, as well as the maintenance of security and stability by emphasizing the role of the military in protecting the homeland and the military's contribute to building and developing the country.

The Charter puts emphasis on the development of an educational system, that helps in the promotion of a national culture primarily concerned with production and linked with technology. In addition to strengthening the Jordanian economy and moving towards comprehensive development, The charter also tackles the issue of Jordanian Palestinian relations, describing it as distinctive and special, while seeking to strengthen the Palestinian identity as it does not contradict the Jordanian identity, since it is the solid platform that governs the relationship between all citizens in the Jordanian state. In fact, the protection of the Palestinian identity is beneficial to Jordan and sustains its national homeland security. The charter also tackled many other topics, such as: Arab unity as a main goal in response to the de-facto of division, family, youth, women and children issues, volunteering, as well as media issues, the constraints and rules of political pluralism, the scientific method based on respect for reason and the belief in dialogue, and subjects regarding the Islamic side of the state[1].

Parliamentary life:

Jordan's parliamentary experience started since the establishment, as the first legislative council goes back to 1929, parliamentary life evolved in many stages, where internal and external events played significant roles in that change. As the

---

[1]   **The Jordanian National Charter**, (1991), Amman: a publication of the Ministry of information. **National Charter and democratization in Jordan**, (1997), Amman: Jordan's New Centre.

first Jordanian parliament goes back to the early days of independence, namely 1947 which is the year following the independence of 1946. The parliamentary elections were also restored after 1989, as after denouncing the legal and administrative unification of the two banks of the river Jordan, the reasons leading to the cancellation of parliamentary life no longer applied, and hence, parliamentary life was restored and a public election was held on November 8th 1989 during a severe economic crisis. The election was held using a grouping system for every constituency, where 647 people competed for the eighty seats of the house of representatives, in accordance to the electoral law number 22 of 1986 and it's amendments, and for the first time, women participated in the race for parliament since being given the right to vote and to run the election in 1973. Participation levels were at 61% of those who registered to vote and obtained election cards, and 54% of the total citizens eligible to vote, giving rise to the eleventh house of representatives representing all political forces present on the Jordanian political scene, where the Muslim brotherhood captured 22 seats, and independent Islamists captured 11 seats, bringing the total to a 40% Islamist house of representatives, while the nationalists and the leftists managed to capture 12 seats, and tribal representation retreated, and with this council, the parliament started practicing their duties in legislation and monitoring, and many laws were issued to re-enforce the Jordanian democratic process.

The Jordanian electoral law No. 22 of 1986 was amended where election by group vote was replaced with a (SNTV - Single Non-Transferable Vote) or a one man one vote one constituency system, and was named the (one vote law), according to which the twelfth election was held on November 8th 1993, where Jordanian women managed to capture one seat in the house of representatives, marking the first lady to make it to the house of representatives in the history of Jordan. Most parties and forces were represented in that parliament, yet, the one man one vote one constituency system affected the Jordanian social fabric in certain ways.

As for the thirteenth House of Representatives (1997-2001), the elections were held through a boycott of many political powers: the Islamic Action Front (Muslim Brotherhood), and the Democratic Party of Jordan, Jordan democratic popular unity party, the Nationalist Action party (HAQ), the Jordanian Constitutional front, the Arab Ansar party and the democratic nationalist movement, the boycott was supported by the professional associations (trade unions). The main reason for the boycott was the (one vote law), the presumption that the election's integrity will be compromised, the complex procedures of registering voters, the inequality in administrative divisions compared to the numbers of voters in those constituencies, and even though the Islamic front boycotted the election, independent Islamist ran the election, the turnout was at 55.9% of all registered voters, and the total turnover from all eligible voters

45%. The thirteenth parliament was dissolved with a royal decree in the summer of 2001 not long before the end of its constitutional term, and parliamentary life was suspended for two years based on the constitutional rights of the king to postpone the elections for reasons that prohibit the holding of an election. whereas the king justified the delay with the complex administrative work in creating magnetic identity cards, while others suggest the reasons may be the political instability to the east (Iraq) and west (Palestine) of Jordan, and their impact on the Jordanian state.

A provisional (temporary) electoral law number 34 of 2001, was the law that the election of June 17 2003 was based upon, forming the fourteenth house of representatives, this law increased the number of seats for the house of representatives from 80 to 110, a women's quota of six seats was allocated, and the kingdom was divided into 45 constituencies across 12 governorates. In addition to the three badeyah areas in the north, middle and south of the kingdom, and on November 20th 2007, the election to form the fifteenth house of representatives was held under the same law of 2001, where participation levels reached 58% of registered voters. A provisional (temporary) electoral law number 9 of 2010 was issued and was named the (virtual constituencies law), using which the election for the sixteenth house of representatives was held, the law also increased the number of house seats from 100 to 120 deputies.

The electoral Law No. 25 for the year 2012 was issued along with the amended law number 28 of 2012 on July 25 2012, the law raised the number of seats of the house from 120 to 150, 108 of which are dedicated to local constituencies, 15 as the women's quota, and 27 for the general constituency using the closed relative grouping system. Under this law, the kingdom is divided into 45 local constituencies, and one general constituency for the whole kingdom, every voter is able to cast two votes, one for the local constituency and the other for the general kingdom wide constituency, an independent committee was formed to oversee the election and to manage the electoral process at all stages through a law named the independent electoral committee law number 11 of 2012, the law was issued on April 9th 2012, where the following table clarifies the evolution of parliamentary life in the kingdom since independence.

The Eighteenth council's elections in 2016:

Based on the Election Act No. 6 of 2016, which relied on the open-list method, the list should include a minimum of 3 candidates and not more than the number of seats assigned to the constituencies. Voters cast their votes on one list and then vote for each candidate on the list, and according to the system promulgated by law on 22/5/2016, the kingdom was divided into 23 constituencies with 130 seats, of which the total number of members of the House of Representatives, including 15 seats for women's quota, 9 seats for Christians and 3 seats for the Caucasus and Chechnya.

The nomination of 2252 candidates, 252 were women candidates, and the competition was so high as to compete with 9.6 per cent for each seat. Elections were held on 20/9/2016 and the number of eligible voters approximately 4.25 million, a million and half have participated with a total percentage of 37.1%. At the governorate level, the capital registered the lowest turnout reaching 23.5%, and the highest in the southern desert, reaching 83.39%. Jordanian women got five seats over the women's quota on the 15 seats, and was represented in the 18th Parliament with 20 seats.

Table No.1: The Kingdom's Polling Rates

The Kingdom	37.1%
Amman	23.5%
Irbid	43.1%
Balqa	42.79%
Karak	65.35%
Ajlun	61.68%
Jarash	59.5%
Mafraq	49.53%
Madaba	48.8%
Zarqa	25.93%
Tafiela	61.94%
Ma' an	50.68%
Aqaba	43.63%
Northern Desert	70.43%
Central Desert	71.89%
Southern Desert	83.39%

Source: Ministry of Interior- Amman- 2016

Table No.2: Houses of representatives

House number	No. of members	Formation date	Date of term expiry dissolution	Reasons of or dissolution
First	20	October 20th 1947	January 1st 1950	For an election for both river banks
Second	40	April 20th 1950	May 3rd 1951	lack of cooperation with the executive power
Third	40	September 1st 1951	June 22nd 1954	lack of cooperation with the executive power
Fourth	40	October 17th 1954	June 26th 1956	lack of cooperation with the executive power
Fifth	50	October 2nd 1956	October 21st 1961	Constitutional term expired
Sixth	60	October 2nd 1961	October 17th 1962	lack of cooperation with the executive power
Seventh	60	Nov. 27th 1962	April 20th 1963	No endorsement for the government
Eighth	60	July 8th 1963	Dec. 23rd 1966	lack of cooperation with the executive power
Ninth	60	February 18th 1967	Nov. 23rd 1974	Ribat summit outcomes
Tenth	60	January 16th 1984	July 30th 1988	The denouncement of the unity of the banks of the river Jordan
Eleventh	80	November 27 1989	March 7th 1993	To pave way for the next election

Twelfth	80	1993	September 1997	To pave way for the next election
Thirteenth	80	November 29 1997	June 2001	Dissolved and suspended for 2 years in accordance with article 73 of the constitution
Fourteenth	110	June 17 2003	August 20th2007	Constitutional term expired
Fifteenth	110	Nov. 20th 2007	Nov. 24th 2009	To pave way for the next election
Sixteenth	120	November 9th 2010	March.2010	dissolved for the Elections
Seventeenth	150	November.2013	May.2016	dissolved for the Elections
Eighteenth	130	September.2016	To date	

Source: Amin, Al-Mashaqbeh, (2007), **parliament in Arab states**, Beirut, PP.106-107, and Amin Al-Mashaqbeh, **Jordanian Political System**, 2017. P 13 Edition.

Political parties Act of 2015:

Political parties act No. 16 of 2015 was issued defining a political party as, "any political organization consisting of a group of Jordanians formed in compliance with the constitution and the provisions of the law in order to participate in public life, and to achieve goals related to political, economic and social affairs, working by legitimate and sound means." And in its fourth article, the law establishes the right to form political parties and permits the voluntary membership in such parties in accordance with the constitution and the provisions of this law, A political party may also participate in the parliamentary election from any location and at all levels. In its fifth article it establishes that political parties may be formed provided that they are established based on equality between all Jordanians and the commitment to democracy and respect for political pluralism. The party cannot be founded on the basis of religion, sectarianism, ethnicity, class or on the basis of racial discrimination or based on origins. Article six of the law tackles the issue of the number of founders, the law states that: The number of founding members may not be less than 150 founding member [1] must meet certain criteria the most important of which:

1) Must be a Jordanian since at least ten years.
2) Have completed twenty-one years of age.
3) Should not be convicted of a felony by a competent court in a case breaching a person's honour or general morality, (except for crimes of a political character) unless the morality status has been restored.
4) Must enjoy moral and legal competence and to be a resident of the Kingdom.
5) To be normally a resident in the Kingdom.
6) Does not claim the nationality of another state or any foreign protection.
7) Should not be a member of any political party or organization be it Jordanian or non- Jordanian.
8) Must not be affiliated with the armed forces, security services, or civil defence.
9) Must not to be a judge.

---

[1] A committee is formed in the ministry of interior called the "Political party Affairs Committee" to consider applications for establishment and to follow up on relevant affairs, headed by the Interior Minister and the membership of Chief of Staff of legislation and the Secretary General of the Ministry of Justice, the Secretary General of the Ministry of Interior, a member of a civil society organization named by the Prime Minister, Commissioner-General of human Rights.

Article 18 of that law establishes eighteen as the minimum age for membership in any established political party, along with the conditions set forth in Article six except for items (2 & 5), in addition to registration and licensing procedures that must be done through the Political Parties Affairs Committee at the Ministry of Interior[1], registered along with what is contained in the manifesto of the political party as well as its slogan, its principles, the criteria for membership eligibility, procedures of forming committees and the choice of leadership, determining funding sources and resources of the party, defining the procedures of dissolution and merger with other political parties, as well as adhering to the principles of the Jordanian Constitution and this law. Political parties are prohibited from using public, charitable, religious or educational institutions or trade and professional unions, The law also gave the right to appeal the Minister's decision if the ministry refuses to announce the establishment of the party during the period stipulated by this Law, for a party that fulfils the conditions set forth in articles of this law, Article (13) stipulates that if the number of founders drops below the five hundred threshold before the announcement of the establishment of the party for any reason, the request is automatically void and invalidated. The Act provides that the party's headquarters, documents, and correspondence, and its means of communications are safeguarded, not be monitored or raided or confiscated except with a legal warrant, the inspection of any political party's headquarters is prohibited unless supported by a warrant from the general prosecutor, exceptions to that are cases of flagrante delicto. The law gave a political party the right to accept donations from Jordanian citizens only, provided that those donations are publicized, and that no more than fifty thousand Jordanian dinars are donated by one person per annum. Article (28) states that a portion of the national budget must be allocated to support political parties from the treasury, according to regulations specifying how grants are distributed or forfeited, and methods of disbursement under a regulation issued for this purpose. The law also provides that citizens are not to be interrogated or held accountable or deprived of his constitutional rights on the grounds of his or her political party affiliations, and sets punishment for whoever violates this. A political party must comply with and abide by the following principles and rules:

1. Compliance with the provisions of the Constitution and respect for the rule of law.
2. Commitment to the principle of political pluralism in ideology, opinion and organization.

---

[1]   Amin, Al-Mashaqbeh, **IBID,** PP.312-318.

3. Commitment to maintain the independence and security of the homeland and the dedication to national unity. And to renounce all forms of violence and discrimination among citizens.

4. Commitment to the principles of equal opportunities for all citizens if the party comes into authority. 5. Commitment to not maintain or create any financial ties with any non-Jordanian person or organization.

5. Refrain from deliberately attracting members from the ranks of the armed forces and the security services, and refrain from the establishment of military or paramilitary organizations.

6. Refrain from interfering with the affairs of other countries, and refrain from compromising the Kingdom's relations with other political states.

7. Maintain the neutrality of public institutions towards the general public in the execution of its functions. The issuance of this law was followed by the revocation of the Political parties Law No. 19 of 2007.

Political parties (2018): Stages of development of the political life since 1992 up to present day1: Upon the issuance of Jordanian Parties Law No. 32 for the year 1992, political parties came back as part of the return to democratic life. On the basis of this law, political parties were official, reaching a count of 26 political parties, this number however decreased by the year 2000 to 23 political parties, and increased to 24 political parties in 2001. In 2006, there are 36 registered political parties, and upon the release of the political parties' act of 2007, the number of political parties that have managed to meet the requirements was 14 political parties, and in 2012, the number of political parties increased to 23 political parties[1].

Political parties are mostly one of more political positions, the nationals, leftists, Islamists and moderate conservatives.

First - national parties:

The focus of this type of party is on the principles and philosophy of Arab unity, and the eternal Arab message, as well as freedom and socialism, and stems from the principle that the Arab world is an indivisible economical and political unit, This type of political party is represented by: The Arab baath Socialist Party, and the Arab Baath Progressive Party, the National Action Front.

---

[1]   Ameen, Al-Mashaqbeh, IBID, P.320

Secondly - leftist parties:

The focus of this trend revolves around the ideas and principles of the Marxist ideology, such parties have modified their principles to suit the Jordanian constitution and the political parties act, leftist parties in Jordan are: The Jordanian Communist Party, The People's Democratic Party of Jordan (HASHD - a backronym meaning crowd in Arabic), the Jordanian Democratic Popular Unity Party, and The Nationalist Movement Party for direct democracy.

Thirdly - Islamist Parties:

Such parties focus on the Islamic religion as a system of principles, ideas, and programs to find solutions to social problems, and calls for the application of Islamic law in various walks of life. Three parties represent this type of party in Jordan: the Islamic Action Front, "which represents the vast majority of the Islamic movement and is supported by the Muslim Brotherhood, an influential and popular group", another such party is The Arab Islamic movement (doaa - which is a backronym for prayer), and the Islamic Centrist Party.

Fourthly - centrist conservative parties:

Sometimes called the liberals (Liberal capitalists), which are mostly close to the governing system. Such parties are usually based on general principles concerning the state that are not unified among such parties, for example, dedication and faith in democracy, political pluralism, public freedoms, and preserving the national identity, national unity, women's rights and social justice, the advancement of the economy and society, such parties include: national Constitutional Party, the national Movement Party, the Reform Party, and United Jordanian front Party.

Table No. 3: List of Political Parties in Jordan (2018)

No.	Party Name	No.	Party Name
1	The Islamic Action Front	2	Jordanian Islamic Center Party
3	Jordanian National Democratic Rally Party (Twad) Party	4	Jordanian Arab Socialist Ba'ath
5	Jordan National Loyalty(Wafa) party	6	Al Balad Al Amen Party
7	Shura Party	8	Jordanian Social Justice Party

9	Al Ansar party	*10*	Jordanian National Action Front party
11	Alshahama party (Magnanimity)	*12*	Jordanian Equality Party
13	Jordan Stronger Party	*14*	Jordanian Arab Party
15	Jordanian Furssan Party	*16*	Jordanian Reform and Renovation party (Hasad)
17	National Unity Party	*18*	Jordan Justice and Reform Party
19	Jordanian Democratic People's Party (Hashd)	*20*	National Aid party
21	Jordanian National Youth Party	*22*	Freedom and Equality Party
23	Jordanian National Current Party	*24*	Jordanian National Union Party
25	Jordanian United Front Party	*26*	Al Resalah Party
27	Nationalist Movement Party	*28*	Jordanian Democratic Popular Unity party
29	Jordan Reform Party	*30*	Jordanian Progressive Arab Ba'ath Party
31	Jordanian National Party	*32*	Jordanian Justice and Development Party
33	Al Hayat Jordanian Party	*34*	Jordanian National Constitutional party
35	Jordanian Social Democratic	*36*	The Jordanian Democratic Nature Party party
37	Al Mustaqbal (Future) Party	*38*	Jordanian Covenant Party
39	. Al-Ahrar Party	*40*	Jordanian National Trend Party
41	Conservative Party	*42*	National Revival Front Party
43	Jordan Promise Party.(Al waad)	*44*	Popular Action Party
45	Al Nidaa' Party	*46*	Al Raya Party
47	National Congress Party(Zamzam)	*48*	Change and Modernity Party
49	Jordanian Communist Party		

Source : Ministry of political Development, Amman 2017.

Financial disclosure law for the year 2006:

The Financial public disclosure law No. 54 of 2006 stipulates in Article number two that the head of the Senate, the Speaker of the House, members of both Houses, the Prime Minister and his Ministers and anyone appointed by royal decree must provide a statement of assets for himself, his spouse and any minors among his or her children within three months of the date he or she is handed the forms of financial disclosure.

Article six of this law states that any assets or property are considered illegitimate whether movable or immovable, as well as any benefit or the right to a benefit obtained by a person whom this law applies to if they are obtained by using his or her position or status, whether such illegitimate benefit or assets was obtained for him, or for any other party, and if such a person's assets, or the assets of his spouse or to his children that are minors increase and he or she fails to clarify a legitimate source for such assets, such assets are considered to be obtained via illegal means using that person's position or status.

The Financial disclosure law No. 54 of 2006 was issued on 1/11/2006 to cover members of the executive branch and the legislature (both Senate and House of Representatives). The law stipulated that it shall come into effect within 1 month of the date of its publication in the Official Gazette, requiring each member of the legislative authority to disclose his or her financial state in both movable and immovable property and assets, as well as a similar statement for his or her spouse and their children who are still minors.

Integrity and Anti-Corruption Commission, 2016:

The Integrity and Anti-Corruption Commission was formed under Law No. 62 of 2006, the law establishes that the Anti-Corruption Commission is linked to the prime minister by the act No. 13 of 2016. The government change the name to become Integrity and Anti-Corruption Commission, where the commission is composed of a president and six members, the commission is responsible for setting and implementing and establishing effective policies to counter corruption and to prevent it, and to detect corruption of all natures, including financial corruption, administrative corruption, and the employment based on nepotism and favouritism in cases where they undermines the rights of others, and to preserve state money, and to provide the foundations of equal opportunity, equality, and justice, and to counter character assassination.

The following are considered corruption, Crimes undermining the duties delegated to a person as stated by the Penal Code, crimes affecting public trust mentioned in the Penal Code, economic crimes within the meaning of the law, compromising public funds, abuse of power in violation of the provisions of the law, and to commit acts of nepotism or favouritism that eliminate a right or wrongfully entitle someone to something, and all the acts of corruption contained in international conventions that the kingdom has been a part of. The law gave immunity to the President and members of the Board except in the case of flagrante delicto or prior permission from the Judicial Council.

These laws adopt effective penalties and effective implementation Techniques. Article 11 of the Law of financial disclosure states: Punished by temporary hard labour whoever obtains unlawful benefits for himself or for others and a fine equivalent to the enrichment and the return of the equivalent of the enrichment. In the case the lawsuit is voided by the death, the return of the enriched money still holds during the two years following the date of death. The law stipulates that, failing to disclose (without a lawful excuse) shall be punished by imprisonment or a fine, or both for any person whom article two of this laws is applicable, despite being notified. The Anti-Corruption Commission has been given the right of law enforcement for the purposes of carrying out their duties.

According to the Commission's report for the different years of 2011-2013, the Commission dealt with 1808 complaints, 1151 of them was filed, and the rest has been transferred to the competent authorities (the judicial authority) or the State Security Prosecutor. And through consideration of the Indicators of corruption of transparency international, the Jordan location is declining; Jordan has declined from 49 to 50 at the international level.

Constitutional Court:

The Constitutional Court Act No. 15 of 2012 was issued on 06.07.2012, and called the law of the Constitutional Court, and the law states in Article two, paragraph (A). A constitutional court is to be established in the kingdom based in the capital Amman, and is an independent judicial body. Paragraph (b) of the same article states that this court has a legal personality and financial and administrative independence, and may own movable and immovable property, and perform all the necessary actions required to allow it to function, and acting on its behalf is the civil attorney general. According to the text of Article four, this court is concerned with the following:

- **First**: overseeing the constitutionality of laws and regulations in force.
- **Second**: interpreting the provisions of the Constitution. Article five of the Constitutional Court Act requires that the king appoints members and presidents of the court for six non- renewable years, noting that when this law comes into force, nine members including the president are appointed in addition to three members that are appointed every two years from the date of the appointment of the nine members. The conditions for membership in the Constitutional Court are as follows:

1. A Jordanian who does not have the nationality of another country.
2. To have reached the age of fifty years (50 years old).

3.   To be of the following categories:

* First: Judges who have served in the Appellate Courts or the higher court of justice.
*Second: of law professors in universities, who hold the rank of professorship.
*Third: lawyers who have spent a period of not less than fifteen years in the legal profession.

The law states that one of the members of this court must be an expert that meets the membership requirements of a senator, and is at least fifty years of age. The law also provides that this member must be fully dedicated to the post and may not hold other public positions and may not practice commercial activity and cannot be part of any board of directors of any company or entity, and shall not be affiliated with any political party, and is subject to financial disclosure law, members of the constitutional Court must take an oath before his Majesty the King.

The right to appeal directly to the Constitutional Court on the constitutionality of laws and regulations is exclusively in the hands of the House of Representatives, the senate, and cabinet of ministers.

The constitutional court requires that appeals be provided within 120 days, this and it is permissible for any party involved in a lawsuit pending at any court type or level to question the constitutionality of a law or regulation applicable to the merits of the dispute. The appeal must be handed to the court handling the lawsuit that prompted such an appeal, and therefore, citizens are not entitled to appeal directly to the Constitutional Court if they have any appeals relating to the constitutionality of laws or regulations.

This Act provided that the court has the right to interpret the provisions of the Constitution if requested to do so by a decision of the Council of Ministers or a decision from either the House of Representatives or the senate taken with a majority vote, and its decision shall be effective after its publication in the Official Gazette.

Court sits to consider the appeal or request for interpretation with a committee of at least nine members. The General Committee of the Court is made up of all its members. The committee is responsible for preparing the annual report on the court's function and for submitting that report to the king, and to sign contracts and agreements of which the court is a party, and to set necessary instructions to organize the work of the court the code of conduct for members of the court. The court makes its decisions with a two-thirds majority vote of the attending members. A Secretary General is appointed to execute the administrative and financial matters, as well as to sign contract on behalf of the court, setting the organizational structure of the Court, and the administration of the financial and administrative systems of the court, the court's accounting is subject to the supervision of the Audit Bureau. Thus, the formation of the Constitutional Court in the Kingdom is a quantum leap in the process of political reform, as the Constitutional Court is the independent supreme judicial reference to the political system, and is a main component of the body and structure of the system for monitoring the constitutionality of laws and regulations, as well as the interpretation of texts and constitutional laws when disputes between the executive and legislative branches arise over the constitutionality of laws. Since 2013 until 2014, judgments of the Constitutional Court have been issued, where 12 decisions were made on unconstitutional laws and defences received in the same period there were 13 interpretive decisions, and in 2015 the Constitutional Court issued one interpretative decision concerning the interpretation of the articles 120-121 of the Constitution.

Independent Elections Commission:

The Independent Election Commission ACT No. 11 for the year 2012 was issued on 09.04.2012, which provided for the establishment of an independent body called the "Independent Elections Commission", the commission enjoys legal personality and financial and administrative independence, and has the right to own movable and immovable property and carry out all necessary legal actions to achieve its goals, Headquarters of the Independent elections commission shall be in the capital (Amman), and the commission has the right to open branches or offices in governorates of the Kingdom[1].

The terms of reference of the Independent Election Commission are to oversee the parliamentary electoral process, and to manage the process in all its stages, or in other words, the direct supervision on the election of the house of representatives, The commission also has the right to oversee any other election set by the Council of Ministers in accordance with the provisions of the legislation in force, and the commission must take all necessary measures whether decisions or actions enabling it to undertake its responsibilities with integrity, transparency, and neutrality, while ministries and governmental institutions must provide all sorts of support to help achieve the committee's tasks and functions in accordance with the provisions of the legislation in force, Ministries and government institutions must also provide the election commission with any documents or information the commission deems necessary to conduct its work. The Commission also works in liaison with the Ministry of Interior to set security plans to ensure the smooth running of the electoral process, the safety of electoral headquarters and polling and counting

---

[1]   Independent Election Commission law No. 11 of 2012 Article 3.

stations, and to maintain the security and safety of voters, candidates, observers and all those related[1].

This body shall have a Board of Commissioners of a chairman and four members, appointed by a Royal Decree for a period of six years non-renewable[2]. The Authority shall have a secretary-general appointed by a decision of the Board of the Commission; the secretary-general's services are also terminated with a decision of the board, provided that the appointment of the secretary-general is associated with a royal decree. The conditions for membership in the body are: to have the Jordanian citizenship for at least ten years, to enjoy full civil capacity, not to have the citizenship of another state, must at least possess a first university degree, should not be a member of the national assembly, must be at least forty years, to be experienced and to possess the know-how, to be known for his integrity and good reputation, not to be convicted of any offense relating to morality, public morality, compromised honor or honesty, or any felony regardless of being legally discharged or included in an amnesty, and should not be affiliated with any political party, the Commissioner and the Secretary-General must be dedicated to the commission on full-time basis, must not conduct commercial business, must not be part of a board of directors for any company, and must not be employed for pay to any party regardless of its status. The commissioner is sworn the constitutional oath before the King[3].

The Council of Commissioners of the Independent election Commission practices the following powers and functions:

1. Sets the general policy of the Independent Election Commission.
2. Set the polling date after the issuance of the king's command to conduct the election for the House of Representatives.
3. Adoption of the schedule plans and programs necessary to implement the electoral process with integrity, transparency and impartiality.
4. Take the necessary measures to register voters and candidates in accordance with the provisions of the election law, to audit records of voters, and to update and handle relevant objections.
5. To publish the records of voters on the commission's website or via any other media specified by the election law.
6. Development of rules for promotion and electioneering campaigns and their procedures, to monitor such campaigns in accordance with

---

[1] Independent Election Commission law articles 4 and 5.

[2] Article 6 of Independent Election Commission law appointed by His Excellency Mr. Abdul Ilah Khatib, president and membership of HE Riyad Shakaa, HE Mohammed Ali Alawneh, HE Atif Btoush, and Mr. Eid Joaed.

[3] Independent Election Commission law, article 8 and 9.

executive regulations, and to raise public awareness of the importance of participation in political life, including the electoral processes.

7. The appointment of chairmen and members of committees for the implementation of the parliamentary electoral process in accordance with the election law, and to set criteria for accepting representatives of candidates at polling stations and counting stations.

8. The adoption of specifications for ballot boxes and ballot papers and the official stamps of the ballot committee.

9. Adoption of representatives of civil society organizations, local and international observers, and media to observe the electoral process and to monitor it.

10. To extend the voting period in accordance with the provisions of the election law.

11. Develop executive regulations to publish preliminary results and organize objection procedures in accordance with the provisions of the election law.

12. The announcement of the final results of the elections.

Part of the board of commissioners' terms of reference is the issuance of the final detailed report covering the entire electoral process in all stages and submitting it to the king, and to publish it in the official gazette. and to publish the annual report on the activities of the Commission and its work, and to send a copy of the report to each of the Council of Ministers and the national assembly, and the formation of temporary specialized committees for specific tasks, and to propose draft legislation necessary for the work of the Commission[1].

The commission may also submit opinions on any proposal to a law relevant to any electoral process and to submit such opinion to the council of ministers[2], the Council takes its decisions by a majority of three votes at least, no member may abstain from voting, but may record the disagreement and sign it in the minutes of the meeting, article 23 of the Act provides that decisions of the Commission on the parliamentary electoral process are subject to appeal before the competent court in accordance with the Constitution and the electoral law in force.

---

[1] Article 12 of the Independent Election Commission Law No.11 for the year 2012.

[2] Article 19 of the Law Independent Electoral Commission No.11 for the year 2012.

Decentralization:

Law No. 49 of 2015, named the Decentralization Law of 2015, follows the law of the ministry of the interior and its administrative provisions. Article 3 of the Law provides that The governor, in addition to the tasks and powers granted on him by the valid legislation, shall undertake the following:

1- To lead the official agencies of the governorate and supervise the discharge of their duties, follow up the execution of state public policy in the governorate, and take the necessary steps to ensure these policies, and applying the laws, regulations, and hold regular meetings for councils and committees chaired by governorate.

2- Coordination between the governorate Council and the municipalities in the governorate and ministries and government departments and public institutions.

3- Supervising development and service plans and to prepare the annual budget for the province and take the necessary measures to ensure that the decisions of the governorate council are implemented and submitted to the competent authorities and work to provide the best services to citizens in coordination with the council.

4- Working with the council and the executive council to provide the appropriate environment to encourage investment in the governorate and to provide the requirements for economic and social development.

5- Maintenance and development of State property, and take the necessary measures to protect health, public safety and the environment; formulate monitoring and inspection committees to monitor all the enterprise and take necessary measures in cases of emergency and coordinate efforts of all competent authorities.

6- Public security forces, gendarmerie, and civil defence forces shall be deployed in the governorate and their centres shall be designated and cancelled in agreement with the governor. The governor can ask the prime minister's support from the Jordanian Armed Forces/ Arab Army when the public security force is insufficient in the governorate.

Article 6:

Every governorate shall have a council called the governorate council, composed of a number of members and it shall have the legal personality with financial and administrative independence; their number are determined in regulations that shall be issued for that purpose; an additional 10% of the number of seats allocated for the elected council's members shall be allocated for women to be filled by the candidates; and the council of ministers appoints 15% of the number of elected members as members in the council, provided that one third of this percentage is allocated to women. The term of the council shall be four years beginning from the announcement of the names of the winners in the Official Gazette. Its term shall end with the end of this interval or in the event of its dissolution pursuant to this Law. The council shall undertake the following duties:

1- Endorse strategic and action plans related to the governorate, referred to it by the executive council and ensure their implementation.

2- Endorse the governorate's draft budget within the limits set by the Ministry of Finance referred to it by the executive council, finding out the means of implementing the annual budgets of all the governorate's municipalities; and approve the governorate's guide of needs in terms of development and service projects referred to it by the executive council and identify the priority needs.

3- Approve the services and investment projects referred to it by the executive council after completing the necessary procedures and endorse development projects of public benefit to the governorate, provided consideration is given to development projects proposed by municipal councils and official departments and institutions within the governorate, and submit them to the governor to take appropriate action in their regard and discuss reports on the implementation of projects, plans and programs that are being caried out by the government departments in the governorate.

4- Propose the establishment of investment projects and carry out joint projects with other governorates with the approval of the competent entities and Put recommendations and proposals for the competent entities that would guarantee enhancements in the performance of government departments and public institution within the governorate to ensure the best in service provision.

5- Identify the areas within the boundaries of the governorate that are suffering from shortages in services and development or have urgent problems, propose appropriate solutions and Composition of the competent committees of members to fulfil the specific functions and powers of the Council by law.

6- Consider any issue submitted by the governor. We believe that the governorate councils within this Law constitute only an advisory body to the governor and the executive council and it can be termed centralized decentralization.

Second topic: Rights and public freedoms in Jordan
Introduction:

In the matter of human rights, human nature and his existence necessitates special considerations, and human rights have evolved throughout the ages to become a global issue, because of which many conventions and international declarations have been issued, creating an international consensus on the matter, yet, there is a big difference between theory and practice, varying between nations that have advanced on this front by setting and implementing mechanisms to support those rights, while others are still struggling to develop such mechanisms. According to John Locke, Fundamental human rights are "life, liberty and property" and from here we can further divide those into the human's right to protect himself/ herself, the right to self-determination, the right to agree or disagree (peace and war), right to expression and his/her social, economical, and political rights. Scholars agree that the origin of rights are natural rights that are enshrined in the natural law, and with society's evolution came the evolution of political power, and with the later came the positive law, which gave rise to civil rights and political rights, where civil rights are defined as rights that humans are born with, such as the right to live, the right to believe, the right to think, the right to marry, the right to form a family (right to reproduction), and the right to own property, and political rights, such as: the right to vote and the right to political participation of all kinds, the right to work in public administration, and the right of conscription (military service). The Jordanian Constitution regulated public freedoms and rights of citizens in many of its articles, where the second chapter was dedicated to those rights and liberties, as we will see from the text of the constitution here.

1 - The right to life:

Article seven of the Constitution provides that personal freedom is protected, and as we can see, the source of freedom in the Jordanian state is the constitution, where throughout the text of the constitution, personal freedom is both respected and honored, as well as a person's dignity, life, livelihood, and safety, where every assault on the rights and public liberties or privacy of Jordanians is a crime punishable by law.

2 - The right to security:

Article (8) of the Jordanian constitution states that "No person may be detained or imprisoned except in accordance with the provisions of the law." and Article (9) of the text of the constitution states: A - No Jordanian may be deported from the territory of the Kingdom. B - No Jordanian may be prevented from residing at any place, or be compelled to reside in any specified place, except in the circumstances prescribed by law, while Article (10) of the Jordanian constitution states that "Dwelling houses shall be inviolable and shall not be entered except in the circumstances and in the manner prescribed by law[1]". It is clear from these constitutional provisions that the Jordanian constitution guarantees the right to security and a decent life and tranquility to all citizens without the slightest fear, and that a Jordanian citizen may not be held or imprisoned except in accordance with the law, and it is well known that the judiciary caries out the law in cases of violations, Jordanian citizens also enjoy the security of not being deported or held in house arrest without a legal justification through a law carried out by the judiciary, You can also note that such texts are in line with international legitimacy.

3 - The right to move and travel:

Article nine of the Constitution provides that Jordanians may travel anywhere within the kingdom, and from the kingdom and back to it, as well as the freedom to settle in any place of their choice, where this freedom may not be restricted unless restricted by provisions of the law.

4 - The right to equality:

Article six of the Jordanian constitution has established the principles of legal equality between all Jordanians, concerning their rights and duties, regardless of race, language or religion, and the defense of the motherland, its unity, and its people's unity, and the maintenance of social peace is a sacred duty to every Jordanian, and that family is the basis of society and its basic building block, and hence, the protection of motherhood, childhood, the handicapped, and the senior citizen. The Constitution also provides for the principle of equal opportunity for all Jordanians, and by looking at the different constitutional provisions, one can see the emphasis on legal equality as there is no discrimination between Jordanians, in addition to the principal of equal opportunity to achieve social equality between citizens, as well as the right to hold public administration positions and government jobs, without discrimination and within the framework of qualifications and competencies, in addition to the use of public facilities for all citizens without favouring or discrimination, the Constitution also guarantees the right to litigation by stating that courts are open to all, and guaranteed to be free of interference, and the

---

[1]   Article 9and 10 of the Jordanian Constitution.

equality in paying taxes, so In short, we can summarize the principals of equality that aim to achieve social justice and non-discrimination between Jordanian citizens as follows:

1. the right to legal equality, Art.6.
2. Non-discrimination among all Jordanian citizens, Art. 6.
3. the realization of the principles of equal opportunities, Art. 6.
4. right to hold public administration positions Art.22.
5. the right to use public facilities, Art.22.
6. Respect for human freedom and dignity, Art. 7, Art. 8.
7. to ensure the right to litigation, Art. 101.
8. equality in taxes and fees, Art.111.
9. the right to address public authorities, Art.17.

5 - The freedom of opinion, belief and worship:

Article (15) of the Jordanian constitution ensures the freedom of opinion and expression in saying, writing, photography, and other means of expression provided that it does not violate the law, and thus, the constitution honors opinion and expression for as long as they do not violate the laws of the kingdom, the constitution also emphasizes that the press and printed material are at complete liberty for as long as they do not violate the law, and that the press cannot be suspended unless certain conditions are met, such as emergencies that are based on constitutional provisions such as article 124 and article 125 for the purpose of maintaining security of the country and protecting it and to maintain law and order within it. Article fourteen of the constitution establishes the freedom of religious belief and religious practice and rituals according to the customs observed in the Kingdom, for as long as they are not immoral and do not violate public courtesy and decency, here we note that religious freedom is a protected right of citizens whether the belief or the rituals provided they do not contradict with the social norm and public decency and moral standards of the Jordanian society.

6 - The right to education:

Article (20) of the Jordanian constitution preserves the right to education and states that elementary basic education is compulsory and free of charge at government schools, and to preserve that right governmental schools are spread in all parts of the kingdom, and for this purpose, Jordanian laws and the Jordanian constitution protect the right to an education, especially the right to elementary compulsory education in government schools in addition to giving people the right to establish schools and to manage such schools as long as such schools are compliant with the law.

7 - **The right to work:**

The Jordanian Constitution states that the state will provide work within its means. And that the state should provide work for Jordanians in order to steer the national economy towards prosperity. The Constitution also makes it clear that the state protects work and issues legislation that adheres to certain principals, some of which are: Every worker shall receive wages proportional to the amount and type of job being done, restricts the weekly work hours, and gives workers paid weekly holidays and paid annual holidays, and specifies compensations for dismissed workers, injured workers, and wherever emergencies emerge due to work functions, and states the terms for women's labour and for the employment of minors, and that workspace is compliant with safety standards, and gives workers the right to organize themselves in trade unions within legal bounds, the constitution also gives all Jordanians the right to hold government positions within the bounds of the rules and regulations of the kingdom, and the adoption of merit and qualifications in scientific and technical fields in employment in those positions.

8 - **Freedom of assembly:**

The Jordanian Constitution gives Jordanian citizens the right to assemble within the limits of the law, and what is meant by this is the meeting of citizens for the purpose of expressing opinions and debating matters, whether through speeches or discussions and debates, and allows them to express their views without violating the laws and regulations, The aforementioned is stated in paragraph (1) of Article (16) stating: "Jordanians shall have the right to hold meetings within the limits of the law".

9 - **Freedom of association and political parties:**

The Jordanian Constitution gives Jordanian citizens the freedom to establish associations and political parties, provided that the purposes are legitimate, with rules of procedure that do not violate the provisions of the Constitution, The constitution also clarifies that the law regulates the establishment of societies and political parties, and monitors their resources, as for charities, law No. (51) for the year 2008 regulates the mechanisms of registration and formation of charitable associations through the Ministry of social Development, as for the political parties law No. (19) for the year 2007 regulating mechanisms of establishing political parties in the kingdom, provided that they are compliant with the constitution and that they have clear and legitimate purposes, as well as using sound means, the above-mentioned political party law defines a political party as: "every political organization consisting of a group of Jordanians formed in accordance with the Constitution and the provisions of the law with the purpose of participation in the political life, and aims to achieve specific goals related to political, economic and social affairs, and functions through legitimate means" the law gave Jordanians the right to voluntarily be affiliated to political parties.

10 - The right to form trade unions and federations:

Article (23) paragraph (f) of the Constitution states that: "Free trade unions may be formed within the limits of the law." meaning that there is a law organizing the work of trade unions of workers, medical practitioners, lawyers, and other professionals, in order to organize the state of an industry, membership to trade unions is compulsory for both workers and professionals, this compulsory condition is needed in order to organize matters that are specific to an industry, and to advance that industry through courses, conferences, and scholarships, as well as the social aspect of compensation, housing, training, pension and similar matters the union provides for its members, and in cases of death or disability, and therefore the freedom to form such trade unions, syndicates, and federations is protected legally and by the constitution.

11 - The right to own property:

Of the fundamental rights is the right to own "property", such that a person can own movable or immovable assets whether in the form of real estate, land, money, or any other belongings, where it was explicitly stated in Article (10) of the constitution as follows "Dwelling houses shall be inviolable and shall not be entered except in the circumstances and in the manner prescribed by law." and Article (11) of the Constitution provides that "No property of any person may be expropriated except for purposes of public utility and in consideration of a just compensation, as may be prescribed by law." and Article (12) stipulates that "No loans may be forcibly imposed and no property, movable or immovable, may be confiscated except in accordance with the law". These three texts protect and safeguard the right to own property, from housing to land to money and property, therefore, the Jordanian political system, through these clear and unambiguous texts respected the right of private property, and that no one's property may be confiscated whether movable or immovable without a judicial judgment based on a law that is effective in the kingdom.

12 - **The right to refuse forced labour:**

The Jordanian Constitution rejects the principle of forced labour for anyone except for certain circumstances as provided by the law, which are emergencies such as war, a general danger such as a fire, flood, famine, earthquakes, dangerous epidemics or any other emergency that can threaten the safety of some or all citizens, and here it is clear that forced labour is forbidden except for certain emergencies or natural disasters for the purpose of protecting society, tranquillity, and public health. In general, the respect for this right that prohibits the imposition of work on individuals for free or so-called "forced labour" except for cases specified by the constitution aiming to protect society in its entirety, protects the freedom of individuals and respects their dignity. The second case provided for by the Constitution that allows for forced labor is the case of a court sentence demanding certain work of a person, or a sentence of service under the supervision of an official authority, provided that this individual is not used for the interest of a third party whether a person, committee, or organization nor can he be put at the disposal of such third party. And here the Constitution makes it clear that even a labor sentence from a Jordanian court must be supervised by an official authority and cannot be administered by any other.

13 - **The right to privacy:**

The Constitution establishes the right to privacy, and the rights of non-interference in an individual's private affairs, except for within the limits permitted by law, as the constitution establishes for the respect for dwelling houses and their privacy by preventing entry, and establishes for the respect of communication privacy be it a mail correspondence, telegram or telephone, as such correspondence may not be wiretapped and can only be monitored within the limits prescribed by law, article (18) of the Constitution states that All postal, telegraphic and telephonic communications shall be treated as secret and as such shall not be subject to censorship or suspension except in circumstances prescribed by law."

14 - **The right to respect for minorities:**

The Jordanian Constitution granted ethnic and religious minorities the right to respect, through article (14) and (19) as it states that the government protects the freedom of religious rituals according with the customs observed in the Kingdom, and granted such groups the right to establish and manage schools for their members taking into account the general provisions prescribed by the law and are subject to government control in their programs. Article (108) deals with Religious community committees and Article (109) on the mechanism of forming such committees[1].

Third topic : Jordanian Foreign Policy

Foreign policy is defined as the advertised work program chosen by official representatives of the international unit among the combinations of alternatives available in order to achieve specific objectives in the international environment[2], and is defined as the organization of the State's activities in its relations with other countries[3]. And also defined as "the group of actions and measures taken by the State related to another state or another group of states in order to achieve its national interest as the first priority, and then move towards other goals[4]".

Jordanian foreign policy decision-making structures:

Structures contributing to Jordanian political Foreign policy are divided into two types, main structures and support structures, and this division relies on whether a structure practices active participation in decision making or influences such decision making, and in what follows, we will try to clarify the role of each of those structures and institutions in forming the foreign policy.

First - the main structure (The King):

Represented by King Abdullah the second personally, who took over his constitutional powers in Jordan on February 7, 1999, Where the Jordanian constitution has delegated many powers, functions and duties that were covered in this book, the King himself carries the planning of foreign policy. as well as

---

[1]   In the field of public freedoms and rights, see the Jordanian Constitution Chapter II. Amin, Al-Mashaqbeh, **IBID,** PP.287-296. The constitutional amendments of 2012.

[2]   Mohamed, El-Sayed Selim, (1984), **Foreign Policy Analysis,** Cairo: Professional Advertising agency, P.16.

[3]   Mahmoud, Khairy Issa and Boutros, Ghali (1979), **An Entry to Political Science,** Cairo: The Anglo-Egyptian Bookshop, P.309.

[4]   Mohamme, Alhazzayma, (1994), **Ideology and foreign policy: a comparative study,** un published Ph.D. Dissertation, University of Tunisia, Tunisia, P.13.

the follow up on issues relating to foreign policy through official visit to other States, and international forums[1].

Secondly - assistive structures in decision-making:

A - The royal court: The royal court is considered the closest of all structures to the king, due to the king's quotidian presence at the royal court to exercise his functions and it is the link between the King and the Prime Minister. the royal court consists of the Chief of the Royal Court and a number of consultants

B - Prime Minister: The King is the one entitled to chooses the prime minister from those who are eligible in terms of qualities and qualifications that fit the current conditions, one who is capable of forming the general policy for the ministers and to speak for the government, the council of ministers caries both internal and external affairs of the state except for what is entrusted to other people or body by the constitution[2], and there is a set role for the prime minister in the formation of foreign policy and contributes to the non-binding advice to the king.

C - The Ministry of Foreign Affairs: The Ministry of Foreign affairs is considered the window that Jordan overlooks the outside world through, as it gathers information from abroad through its consulates, embassies, and missions, and then provides state agencies with information according to every agencies mission and function, and the foreign minister carries an executive role to implement that foreign policy.

D - The military: The military is an executive foreign policy tool, for which the king is the supreme commander, and the defense minister is an executive post who is also a king's adviser in matters and decisions where the military is involved in implementation of such decisions, or where they require secondary military efforts, the King also consults the minister of defense as well as consulting the director of public security and the chief of general intelligence.

E - The legislature: The legislature plays an active role in the discussion on foreign policy, through the Foreign Affairs Committee in addition to the sessions of both houses in general, and makes non- binding

---

[1]   Fouad, Said, (1988), **Jordanian Foreign Policy: A Study of variables**, un published Master Thesis, National Institute of Studies and Socialism, Baghdad, P.155.

[2]   The Jordanian Constitution, Article 45.

recommendations to government, in addition to treaties and agreements that are related to the territory of the State, and treaties that require funding from the treasury require ratification through a law issued by the legislature in accordance with Article 33 of the Constitution.

King Abdullah the second and Foreign Policy:

Ever since king Abdullah the second came into power, he has been trying to devote a new page for Jordan's foreign relations, away from accumulations and disagreements of the past, The king's active presence is clear in his visits and through his contribution and constant attendance of regional and international conferences to serve Arab and Jordanian causes, within a framework of priorities set according to the purpose of attaining legitimate Arab rights in all of the nation's causes. And to create the appropriate atmosphere to enable economic and social development and the creation of economic prosperity, and the transition from modern Jordan to the developed Jordan, His Majesty King Abdullah the second works based on platforms and pillars that illuminate his way and work and these are as follows: -

First: the absolute dedication to the Hashemite heritage, for he is the inheritor of the Hashemite flag through fifteen centuries of the Hashemite message. Respect for tradition, and the system of values that he has been endowed with which has been transferred to him through this timeless message are the guide of his work and orientations. –

Second: His Majesty the King has the religious legitimacy, the historical legitimacy and the political legitimacy, inherited through the rule of the Hashemite dynasty, and the legitimacy of accomplishment, where those legitimacies are a solid base for his positions and orientations on all scales. –

Third: His Majesty the King's commitment to joint Arab action, and the mechanisms to activate and develop it, to make it in line with the variables of our time, for the king is the advocate and leader of Arab solidarity, for he is the chairman of the first Arab summit, and he had a key role in bringing different views closer, and his role in conflict resolution and a role in achieving feasible solutions between Arab states, is but clear evidence of the priority the king assigns to Arab solidarity and his aims to activate it across all fields, for Arab interests were and still are the dominant consideration in his decisions, for he always gives more priority to Arab interests in general over Jordanian state interests. –

Fourth: commitment to the Palestinian cause and the rights of the Arab Palestinian people in the restoration of their territorial integrity and to achieve a just, comprehensive and lasting peace in compliance with the resolutions of international legitimacy, and in compliance to security council resolutions

242, 338 and the resolutions of the United Nations General Assembly related to the Arab - Israeli conflict. And as seen in successive letters of designation of governments, his majesty focuses on standing by our brothers in Palestine and to assist them in reaching their legitimate rights and to help them establish an independent Palestinian state with Jerusalem as its capital. –

Fifth: faith in moderation (mediation) displayed in tolerance, openness to the world, and his sincere faith in the importance of economic, political, and social modernization, by creating atmosphere to attract foreign investment, and the continued focus on the development of human resources, the development of science, and technology transfer, and to build a developed Jordan through the beginning of the third millennium.

Jordanian foreign policy goals:

Jordanian foreign policy goals are set in the light of the supreme national interest, and King Abdullah the second has been working on the achievement of such goals since he assumed his constitutional powers on 7 February 1999, and in short we can say that the Jordanian foreign policy objectives are:

- Maintaining the independence of Jordan and to safeguard its national sovereignty and territorial integrity, and to maintain its national unity, and to ward off all risk and external threat from around the state.
- Development of Jordan's national interests and welfare, and to preserve such interest, and the economic exploitation of national, economical, human resources and to improve the national economy by promoting economic growth, and encouraging investment to enhance national security and stability in all areas.
- To establish for respect of the international community, and to gain credibility, and to promote respect for Jordan, and to advance the good reputation and stability of Jordan's position at the international level. To preserve the existing hereditary monarchy system, and to strengthening popular loyalty, and to deepen the sense of national belonging and its constants, and to enhance the political legitimacy, a legitimacy deep-rooted in the depth of Arab and Islamic history. - Protection of national security and maintaining it through the constant and sincere quest to establish good-neighborly relations with all Arab countries and to invoked the principle of non-interference in the internal affairs of Arab states, and to interact based on the rules of mutual respect, diplomacy, dialogue and understanding to resolve all sorts of disagreements and misunderstandings or misinterpretations of the Jordanian positions on any matter.

- To establish balanced relations with the Western states, in particular the United States, the European Union among other major powers and actors in the international order in order to gain respect and credibility and to employ such credibility and respect to serve the supreme national interests and to serve Arab issues. And to further enhance openness and interaction with international and regional organizations in order to exchange experience and to cooperate in all aspects to further develop the capabilities and potential of the state.
- Seeking to eliminate the sources of territorial dispute in the Middle East and to achieve lasting, just and comprehensive peace to ensure the security and stability of the region, and a commitment to decisions of international legitimacy issued by the United Nations, and to respect signed international conventions, treaties and agreements, and to consider peace as a national strategy.
- Commitment to the principles and ideas of the Great Arab Revolt, calling for unity, independence, freedom, and respect for the charter of the League of Arab States in order to activate the mechanisms of joint Arab action, and the creation of Arab solidarity, and the constant quest to unify Arab stances towards the current issues and challenges.
- To contribute to the strengthening of international peace and security through participation in peacekeeping forces to resolve disputes and provide security and stability, where the presence of several Jordanian armed forces of all forms in various points of tension and conflict the world is but a perfect example and evidence of the Jordanian humanitarian role in global international peacekeeping.
- Combating terrorism in all its forms, and security cooperation with all countries in order to eradicate it.

Fourth Topic: Factors of Political Stability in Jordan

A stable society does not mean that this society does not have any complaints or criticism about the government or the existing regimes, where the sanctity of the law is never violated. Stability in politics is a relative concept that describes the process of the legal and peaceful transfer of power. Stability is linked to the absence of political violence and the existence of a stable political system governed by peace and obedience to the law, and decisions are taken in accordance with the preset procedures.

Historically, Jordan has suffered from different waves of political instability, but the regime was able to maintain its continuity and relative stability, particularly during the Arab Spring and beyond. Therefore, there are several factors that have contributed to enhancing the political stability in Jordan. The character of the King and his political behavior; The role of the military and other security services; The prevailing social structures and the state of social harmony and the centrality of the system during the crises.

In addition, there are two more important factors including the high degree of political adaptation and the rise in the political awareness of the Jordanian citizen. The political conduct of the Hashemite leadership is represented by King Abdullah II, whose legitimacy is grounded on multiple bases including religious legitimacy, national legitimacy (as the leadership of the Great Arab Revolution), and the historic legitimacy of the Hashemite family and its role in the Kingdom and the Arab world. It is known that King Abdullah II has a strong political will of political reform and the development of the structure of the existing political system.

Despite the volatile environment and prevailing economic conditions, the King is proceeding with political reform measures in various aspects. The King is characterized by rationality, wisdom and clarity in dealing with the vocabulary of reform. Accordingly, two main factors of political stability in Jordan will be discussed: the degree of political adaptation of the regime and the high level of political awareness among the Jordanian citizen. Degree OF POLITICAL ADAPTATION Political adaptation is the ability of the political system to adapt to internal and external variables in order to carry on in a viable manner. It is also the process of anchoring the beliefs and values of the basket and belonging to the state.

There is no political system that is capable of perpetuating political life without establishing the minimum common beliefs related to the legitimacy of governance and the importance of the values of the system to the values of the people. This involves building a political culture that is based on the awareness and knowledge of the key terms and vocabulary of the system including the constitution, laws, and main structures of the system, as well as the knowledge, appreciation and respect of the state's key symbols, as well as the ability to criticize the performance of government or performance evaluation, and seek to adapt to the process of mobilizing or creating positive support for the system and its components.

Successful adaptation leads to fortifying the positive support from the people to the authority, which leads to respect for the law bringing a sense of psychological satisfaction and deepening the central values of belonging to the state and promoting national pride. The various patterns of political adaptation include a political system that seeks to achieve stability, create the means to resolve internal conflicts legally, pursue development, modernization and political reform that is a relatively constant renewable political system.

Such a political system provides the main conditions for adaptation beginning with a constitution, constitutional institutions, the ability to meet new needs and demands, and adherence to these demands through the regime to maintain legitimacy thus leading to the continuation of the political system, all the while confirming that these factors support the state of political stability. And we believe that there is an equation linked to success and achievement, which leads to political stability and thus continuity of the system. Those familiar with the political history of Jordan believe that the existing system enjoys a great deal of political adaptation, which has led to relative political steadiness, and therefore the factor of political adjustment is one of the factors of political stability of the state. The process of political reform began before the Arab Spring began in several decades. Since 1989, martial law has been frozen, and the eleventh parliamentary elections were held.

In April 1990, the regime started issuing the National Charter document, which is a political document that clarifies the political process and establishes a general framework for practicing political pluralism and the democratic foundations needed to build a democratic civil society. It is also a comprehensive intellectual and political framework that regulates the relationship between institutions of government and society at all levels. The leadership has sought to institute a new legal system for the Political Parties Law No. 32 of 1992, the Law of Publications and Publication No. 10 of 1992, and other laws that constitute the essence of political adaptation besides the establishment of an independent anti-corruption body in 2006.

This approach has continued despite all the imbalances and difficulties. The Arab Spring has pushed the system to adapt even more to the accelerating changes by making many other reforms, starting with the amendment of nearly 42 articles in the Constitution in 2011, and the establishment of the Constitutional Court based on the law of Court No. 15 of 2012, and the establishment of the Independent Commission for Election Law No. 11 of 2012, and the Political Parties Law No. 16 of 2012. The work of the system of national integrity in 2012, and the government is currently sending a draft law on decentralization of the House of Representatives in its special session held on 1 / 6 / 2015 as well as the amendment of the law of municipalities, and the political parties law draft for 2015.All this leads to the argument that the political adaptation in the Jordanian political system has led to a high degree of political stability, and therefore political adaptation is one of the factors of political stability of the Jordanian state.

Political awareness of Jordanian citizens The political changes that have taken place in the Kingdom over the past two decades have increased the level of public education and higher education, significantly reduced illiteracy levels, and increased mass media coming from the IT revolution (Internet, various media, social media, electronic attitudes, satellite channels, etc.).In addition to this, peaceful democratic transformation and the establishment of a legal system governing democratic life in all its aspects along with the creation of new structures with specific functions, and relatively high levels of freedom, equality, justice and the rule of law have contributed to the high degree of institutionalization in the system and its high capacity for adaptation and containment.

The political awareness of events and issues at all levels has risen to a high degree, and thus the political awareness of the Jordanian citizen is a fundamental factor of political stability of the state. The understanding of the facts of the political reality of the Jordanian situation first in the individual in terms of full knowledge of the economic conditions experienced by the state, and accepting a relatively high cost of living standard, despite the realization of the reality of high prices and inflation and low powers of the national currency against hard currency, and endurance on many of the imbalances. In the administration of weak and low administrative achievement and bureaucracy with its negative and increasing external public debt, and putting up with many negativities to maintain the state of security and stability throughout the Kingdom. The blessing of security and political stability and the absence of factors of instability in the Jordanian situation goes back to the awareness of the individual and the citizen of the situation in all its manifestations and dimensions.

After the occupation of Iraq in April 2003, the Iraqi state fell with all its components, structures and institutions brought by external forces to impose a failed political process that led the Iraqi society towards sectarian war that was fed by many of the internal components and: the absence of political stability and security of Iraq over the past period of time, and with the emergence of jihadist Salafist currents (Daesh) Islamic Radicalism and others increased level Violence, the Iraqi state has become a failure and suffered from the killing, looting, displacement, displacement, corruption, and ongoing conflicts may be longer, and all was in front of the eyes of the Jordanian citizen.

The Arab Spring, which began in Tunisia and quickly spread to Egypt, Libya, Yemen, and Syria, and its after-math affected the Jordanian citizen's mind and level of political awareness. Despite the relative stability that prevailed in Tunisia and Egypt, the most important events affecting the situation in Jordan are the destruction of Syria, the killing, displacement and asylum seekers fleeing to Jordan.

The Jordanian citizen witnessed with his eyes the repercussion in his home country with the influx of Syrian asylum seekers, which exceeded one and a half million in Jordan solely, noting that numbers of refugees in other neighboring countries like Turkey, Lebanon and Egypt have reached over four million citizens. In this period of time, a popular Jordanian movement emerged in many governorates demanding political reform, combating corruption, improving living standards, improving public administration, bringing about general changes in the structure of the state.

The Jordanian peaceful movement was met by a state of high level political adjustment in the gradual response to real political reform, which appeared in the constitutional amendments in 2011 and others, not to mention that the peaceful handling by the security forces and related bodies was a treatment based on containment away from the use of violence or force.

The security agencies at all levels dealt with peaceful civilized methods using the law and the judiciary, to say their fair opinion on most of the cases before them. The wise leadership, led to the decline of the movement in all regions of the Kingdom, and in this regard, was the key in containing the Jordanian movement and facing managing it with the highest standards of objectivity, and responding to what can be achieved within the capabilities and possibilities available.

The events of the region specifically in Syria, Iraq, Yemen, Libya and the continuation of the Palestinian-Israeli conflict have all affected the mind of the Jordanian citizen and the guardian in understanding the value of security and political stability of the state. The external factor and its chaos, killing, destruction, migration and the absence of the values of justice and equity have contributed greatly to the rationality of the citizen's mind, and have increased the awareness of the importance of the concept of comprehensive security.

Furthermore, it has also enhanced their ability to coexist with the newcomers, despite their political consciousness of the internal imbalances and failures. Going back to the causes of political awareness of the citizen, those can be summarized as follows: Education and Literacy The development of education in the Kingdom is remarkable. Since human resources are a fundamental component of the state and its capabilities especially with the absence of natural resources, the citizens aimed at improving their capabilities, and the state has facilitated that by expanding the base of education.

Comparatively speaking, historical sources indicate that the number of students in public and private schools in 1934 were at 11,000 students, whereas today, there are 1.7 million students. Higher education began in 1962 with the establishment of the first Jordanian university that started off with about 340 students, and now there are more than 33 public and private universities with more than 320,000. In addition, there are approximately 28,000 students in vocational and technical education, as well as community, government and private colleges. In addition, the illiteracy rate has declined significantly at a general level of 6.8%. Therefore, education, knowledge and the ability to write and read is an important factor in raising levels of awareness, and political awareness of reality and events is one of the branches of public awareness.

Mass Media Three decades ago, the global revolution in communications and information technology, which swept the whole world, including Jordan, has become more widespread in the last decade. It has affected the rapid changes in the field of information technology, and has become an integral part of the educational system. All levels have become easy to deal with these technological advances. Communication, which increased levels of education and knowledge and expand the perception of the individual. The emergence of satellite and general and specialized electronic sites, the Internet and the means of social communication contributed to the increase of awareness of Jordanian citizens, especially the new generation. Taking into consideration that 53% of the members of the Jordanian society under the age of 20, study in this field, 40% have an Internet subscription and 62% have access to the Internet through their work sites, more than 12 million cellular subscriptions and the development of the media every year, have all greatly enhanced the degree of knowledge and awareness of many issues and events on the internal and external levels through the increased amount of information reaching the citizen. This factor is a major reason for heightened public, as well as political awareness.

The Third Wave of Democracy At the beginning of the 1980s, a third wave of democracy, based on public freedoms, human rights, equity and justice, and the dissemination of basic democratic values such as freedom, justice and equality, human dignity and the rights of women and children emerged. The Jordanian citizen's mind has been influenced by these values and the increasing awareness of the Jordanian citizen. They have become relatively part of the system of public values and are dealt with daily, not to mention the role of the educational curricula and the means of mass communication. In addition to the democratic transformation that the country has undergone since 1989, and what has been achieved in this field in the legislative framework of the law and the renewal of structures. In addition, institutions as well as the slight change in the social value system, to expanding the base of political participation at the national and local levels, have all contributed directly to the increase of the level of awareness of the Jordanian individual.

National Pride (belonging first)The Jordanian people are generally very proud about their homeland and its political system. This is part of the general political culture which depends on three dimensions: the knowledge dimension in the system along with its components, and the evaluation dimension it has on the ability of the individual to evaluate the performance of the institutions of the system positively or negatively. Affiliation is the sense of belonging and peoplehood of the individual to his homeland. It is "the first place and the first" interacting with this place by words, deeds and action and his willingness to stand by this country and defend it. Affiliation is also the sense of belonging to the nation, people and culture.

This is expressed in the "citizenship", and evidenced by the positive participation in all activities of the community and by defending the interests of the country and the sense of pride in this affiliation. It is also the safeguarding of the achievements and public utilities. Moreover, loyalty is that sense of devotion and allegiance to the political system where the individual feels his loyalty to the idea, and believes that he represents and is identical with it. This factor is the essence of Jordanian citizens, who contributed to increase their political awareness and their full responsiveness of maintaining the state of security and stability and by conforming with the principle of existence, while continuing under the umbrella of pride. Moreover, it is known that national pride increases in periods of crises. Therefore, the Jordanian citizen's awareness is high, not to mention that the political system enjoys a very high legitimacy based on historical, religious and national factors and continuous achievement. Based on the foregoing, it is possible to say that a new concept has been carved out as factors of political stability in the Hashemite Kingdom of Jordan, which is the basic awareness of the Jordanian citizen, in addition to other factors.

The phenomenon of political awareness, which is based on understanding, awareness, rationality, prudence, and knowledge of the situation and the event, contributes directly to enhancing the security situation and the relative stability witnessed by the Kingdom. No one can deny this fact today. Although there are imbalances in the social, political and administrative reality, they remain a very minor subsidiary of the overall situation of the country. The phenomenon of political awareness among the people of Jordan throughout the homeland is a cornerstone for the state's political and security stability in the country. Today, we are more capable than ever of protecting and defending the homeland as a result of the national awareness of the importance of preserving the equation of success, and this is all due to the political stability in the Hashemite Kingdom of Jordan.

CHAPTER V

The Royal Discussion Papers

Introduction:

THE PURPOSE OF the seven royal discussion papers is to construct a national intellectual dialogue geared towards democracy enhancement and enrichment of serious national dialogue relating to a number of concepts and values which should be a part of serious national constructions that relates to a number of concepts and values and a part of dialogue and intellectual visions which come in core of the Jordanian scene aiming making a characterized quality translation in political update process.

His majesty the king considers that this methodology a part of responsibility he assumes to encourage serious dialogue among people through democratic transformation channel and development of practices necessary to democracy and progress starting from other opinion respect as a foundation to partnership among all social components and citizenship which becomes complete only via questioning duty practicing and all are partners in sacrifices and earnings. We may disagree but we do not go apart since dialogue and harmony are a continued national duty. His majesty the king seeks through discussion papers to a collective feeling crystallization relates to dignity and pride with what we collectively as a people and development of achievement national feeling inclined to override challenges and participation in Jordan future making in addition to dialogue sustainability and continuity among citizens through all means.

The Royal discussion papers aimed at citizenship concept national belonging focus and enhancement of rule of law pointing out that nobody is above the law and citizenship deepening based on right and duty within their legal framework as effective citizenship. Rule of the law is the foundation of the civil state and political parties, government and citizen in national life.

The seventh discussion papers focused on democratic transition deepening and enhancement parliamentary government methodology and gradual transition towards constitutional royalty by effective citizenship. Generally the discussion papers aimed to create a national dialogue that would result in the creation of a democratic model of various goals, and clarifying the different roles all players in the political process and stations are required to perform in order to transform this model on real grounds. The discussion papers did not ignore protection of multiplicity, progression, and political opportunity justice. The papers talked about achievements that has been realized by now in relation to constitutional amendments and achievement of judiciary package organizing democrati and political life like law amending to state security court and political party election law. In terms of institutional achievements independent election body set up has been made with set up of constitutional law and National Integrity System. Human rights national center and public sector development support was made. Discussion papers outlined that the Hashemite Royalty assumes the responsibilities of making available a leadership methodology collective to all components looking forward for future targeting prosperity realization to nations' generations and protecting our national and domestic security and protection of our religious heritage and social fabric.

1. Our Journey to Forge Our Path Towards Democracy

By Abdullah II ibn Al Hussein 29 December 2012

The Coming Campaign

National lists and candidates across the country have begun their election campaigns for the next Parliament, launching an intense, short election period, in which every day matters, and every citizen matters, because it is your active participation, as citizens, that will breathe life into our democracy. Candidates are not running for the right to sit in Parliament in Amman and earn personal benefits. They are running to be given a responsibility and a privilege: the national duty of making key choices on some of the most important decisions facing our country, decisions that will impact the future of every Jordanian.

My goal and responsibility within this national course is to encourage debate about our progress as a nation in democratic development. This paper is part of efforts towards that goal. Today, and in a series of other discussion papers in the next few months, I seek to stimulate debate among citizens about the most important issues we face as a country. A few weeks ago, in an interview with Al-Rai and The Jordan Times newspapers, I outlined in detail my vision for Jordan's democratic future and the roadmap to get there. Today, I dedicate this paper to share my vision for the principles and values needed to help us progress in our democratization journey, under our constitutional monarchy. Now is the time for us to move actively towards key, practical milestones in that journey towards democracy. This election is one of those critical steps and a station on the political reform roadmap. As candidates come to your neighborhoods over the next several weeks, they will be seeking to win your trust and your vote. But what they need to realize is that they must maintain your trust and honor your vote over the years to come. You have the right and the responsibility, and more importantly a national duty, to engage them in discussion on key issues related to the economy, the country's reform course and your vision for the future of our beloved Jordan. It is equally important that you not only engage the candidates, but engage each other, as citizens, on all issues of priority without restrictions – at home, in coffee shops and community halls, in all gatherings and venues. To make democracy work, it is critical that we debate, discuss, and vote on the basis of the positions put forward by the candidates on key issues facing our country, and not on the basis of personalities or affinities related to geography or family. As groups of citizens – whether in the form of political parties or community groups – we need to embrace political life as a fair and noble competition to generate the best ideas and solutions. No individual or group will get everything it wants. We must strike compromises in order to make the best possible choices in the interest of all Jordanians. The true and decisive test for our nation and our democratization journey is our ability to triumph together as one family in the face of the challenges that come before us. The ideas outlined above require discussing a set of principles that are essential to developing the right practices for democracy. What we all need to develop, starting with the launch of this new election campaign, are the practices of good citizenship that are the foundations for a vibrant and effective democracy, and to work sincerely to guarantee that these practices become our modus vivendi. I believe that there are four practices we must each embrace as citizens to help build our democratic system. While we should start adopting these practices as of this election campaign, that is only the beginning. We will continue to practice and develop these principles in our daily lives over the years to come, because these practices are the sine qua nons for democracy:

I. RESPECT FOR ALL FELLOW CITIZENS IS THE ESSENSE OF OUR UNITY:

We need to acknowledge that as Jordanians we are all fellow travellers in the journey ahead, regardless of family, neighborhood, gender or religious belief. We should engrave in our minds the unshakable fact that our unity and faith in this country transcends all differences. We must expand our circle of trust and respect, and build an inseparable bond between us to treat all fellow Jordanians with civility and dignity, irrespective of whether we know them well or not and whether we like them or not. Respect in the public sphere means that we focus on issues, not personalities, and listen as intently as we talk. We all need to realize that understanding the opinion of others is the most crucial act of respect. There is no such thing as 'free speech' unless we listen. This is how we leave behind 'Us versus Them' ways of thinking, for at the end of the day we are all Jordanians and we are all for Jordan.

II. CITIZENSHIP AND ACCOUNTABILITY GO HAND IN HAND:

I call on all fellow citizens to actively engage in important decisions and problem-solving activities of our society, such as reducing poverty and unemployment, continuously enhancing healthcare and education, improving public transport, overcoming the increasing cost of living, and fighting corruption and any waste of public funds. This starts now, by making our voices heard in the election campaigns and by voting on Election Day. But democracy is much more than voting, and does not end with casting our ballots. It is an on-going process; it is about holding our elected officials to their commitments and remaining continuously engaged in the discussions and debates on the issues facing our families, our communities and our nation. This is why candidates must propose practical, objective and fact-based programs that provide implementable solutions to our challenges, rather than just theoretical slogans and over-diagnosis of our problems. As citizens, I call on you to uphold practices that will keep our society engaged and vibrant. Engaged citizens follow the news in newspapers, online, and on radio and TV. They write letters to the editors of their newspapers or to their Members of Parliament. They join community groups to organize community action about local issues and problems such as playgrounds, traffic safety, rubbish collection, water and sewage networks, and maintenance of roads and infrastructure.

III. HARNESSING DISAGREEMENT INTO COMPROMISE WHILE MAINTAINING CONTSTANT DIALOGUE:

It is important to combine the communication of our own opinions to others with a commitment to disagreeing respectfully with others, as we seek compromise solutions. The diversity of opinion, belief, and culture that exists in Jordan is our fundamental strength, not weakness. Disagreement is not a sign of trouble or disloyalty. Respectful disagreement is the basis for dialogue, and dialogue over diverse ideas is the essence of democracy, and democracy is what makes compromise and agreement possible and will enable our nation to move forward. Compromise means give and take, it means we do not get everything we want, nor does anyone else. The ability to compromise is a virtue. It is not a sign of personal weakness or humiliation. The best and most virtuous citizens among us are those who are willing to accept personal sacrifice in the interest of the nation as a whole, and this is why those who put their country first will remain forever engraved in our hearts and minds. It is equally important that we commit to one another to resolving differences of opinion through debate and dialogue, long before engaging in protest or withdrawing from the discussion and taking to the streets.

IV. SHARED GAINS AND SACRIFICES:

We have to be patient in our understanding that democracy means that there are no permanent winners or losers and no permanent answers. We have to constantly adapt to changing circumstances. Throughout its history, our nation has demonstrated an ability to be agile, accommodate change and adapt as our circumstances require. We all gain from continuing to engage with one another, and continuously striving to move our country further along our development path, armed with the firm belief that we are all partners, both in gains and sacrifices. What I have proposed so far are necessary practices that are crucial for a country seeking democratisation, but it also begs the question: How will we measure progress? As electoral campaigns go on, and through each year of our continuing democratic development after the election, we will know we are on the right path, because we will see ourselves getting better and better at these practices:

- A shared sense of dignity and pride in what we are doing together as a nation;
- A sense of achievement in overcoming the challenges and hurdles we confront together, through shared commitment and shared sacrifice,

on our path to prosperity and greater security through a stronger democracy;

- Active engagement in shaping the future of Jordan through voting in elections – a commitment to democracy as a national paradigm and a way of life;
- Fruitful and respectful debates and discussions taking place in person and online;
- Civility between citizens characterized by a strong volunteering culture and growing generosity and trust to, and from, people we do not personally know.

It is well evident for all that we have embarked on a new and exciting chapter in our nation's development at a time of historic challenges. Moreover, we are passing through a decisive juncture, full of challenges and opportunities, and I remain a firm believer in the ability of Jordanians to overcome challenges and seize opportunities. I look forward to hearing the views and positions of all candidates running in this election. The responsibility assumed by those elected to the new Parliament on behalf of all citizens is enormous. By exercising the practices of good democratic citizenship outlined above, Jordanians are all encouraged to seize the rights granted to them under the Constitution to fully exercise their responsibility to elect a competent new Parliament in the best interest of the nation's future and take part in expressing the will of the people, for they have earned their rightful status as true partners in decision making. Now is the time we must each take responsibility for creating the future we want for all Jordanians by making democracy a way of life.

2. Making Our Democratic System Work for All Jordanians

By Abdullah II ibn Al Hussein 16 January 2013 Democracy is fundamentally something active, something we do as citizens and as a country. In Jordan, the basis for our democracy is the Constitution, which for close to 90 years has provided the framework for how we make public choices and decisions. This is the foundation, but our laws and institutions must continue to evolve and develop. We have made much progress on this path in recent years. We have amended one third of the Constitution and established the Constitutional Court and the Independent Electoral Commission. This enhanced the separation of powers, the checks and balance of our governance system, the independence of our judiciary and the inalienable rights of our citizens. These actions empower the Jordanian people to shape the country's future in a way that is more transparent, fair and inclusive than ever before. Now we need to build on this foundation. Crafting a modern democratic society will be the product of our learning and developing together over time, not a single moment or set of reforms. Reform is not merely a question of changes to laws and regulations. It requires an evolution in how citizens, civil servants and the representatives entrusted to make decisions on behalf of citizens operate and interact within the current system. As I outlined in my first paper, our commitment to active citizenship, respect and accountability, shared gain and sacrifice, and dialogue and compromise along our journey, is critical to our success as a nation. In this paper, I want to discuss another critical aspect of our democratic development – the transition to parliamentary government. The principles underpinning our journey are clear. We will nurture and protect political pluralism and develop the appropriate checks and balances for a properly functioning democracy. We will strengthen and enhance our civil society and ensure a level playing field for political competition. The rights of all citizens, especially those of minorities, will be safeguarded as per our Constitution. The key question we must answer together is how our institutions and systems will continue to enshrine and protect these principles as we make our transition.

The Architecture of Our New Democratic System in Context

The fundamental principle of modern democracy is that the people elect representatives to make important public decisions on behalf of the country as a whole. As countries have developed their democratic systems, a variety of models have emerged for the implementation of this democratic principle. In a republic, for example, there are both presidential and parliamentary systems. In a presidential system (for example, France), the president is elected and can often appoint the government directly, although the approval of parliament may still be required. In a parliamentary system (for example, Turkey), the government is often appointed by a Prime Minister from the elected parliament's majority party or coalition of parties. In a constitutional monarchy, similar to the parliamentary system in a republic, the government is often formed from the elected majority party or coalition of parties in the legislative assembly (much like Spain and Belgium). There are multiple variations on each of these models, and there is no single 'correct' solution for all countries. Each nation's system reflects its unique history and culture. Today, Egypt and Tunisia are evolving republics. Morocco, like Jordan, is a constitutional monarchy. Our constitutional monarchy has changed and evolved for the past nine decades and will continue to do so. The next stage is an evolution in how we select our Government.

The Transition to True Parliamentary Government

As I have said before, the path towards deepening our democracy lies in moving toward parliamentary government, where the majority coalition in

Parliament forms the Government. After the upcoming elections, we will start piloting a parliamentary government system, including how our Prime Ministers and Cabinets are selected. International experience suggests this will require several parliamentary cycles to develop and mature. The key driver of the timeline for this transition is our success in developing national political parties whereby they capture the majority of votes by citizens and with competent leaders capable of assuming positions in our Government. Historically, the Prime Minister and Ministers have been chosen for their leadership qualities and expertise, and approved by a vote of confidence in Parliament. Our Ministries have depended on their knowledge and experience to manage the challenges facing Jordan. Without properly functioning national political parties to develop national platforms and build coalitions, as well as capable of capturing the majority of votes by citizens, it has historically been the exception rather than the rule for the Government to include serving Members of Parliament. However, it is important that we start building our system of parliamentary government. As a first step, we will change how the Prime Minister is designated after this upcoming election.

- The new prime minister, while not necessarily an MP, will be designated based on consultation with the majority coalition of parliamentary blocs.
- If no clear majority emerges initially, then the designation will be based upon consultation with all parliamentary blocs.
- The Prime Minister-designate will then consult with the parliamentary blocs to form the new parliamentary government and agree on its program, which will still have to obtain and maintain the Lower House's vote of confidence.

The Conditions for a Successful Transition

Full parliamentary government depends on the development of three conditions that ensure continued expertise and effectiveness:

First, we will need to see the emergence of true national parties that aggregate specific and local interests into a national platform for action. This will take some time. However, as more seats in Parliament come to be held by political parties that compete nationwide, based on national platforms for four-year programs and then form solid parliamentary blocs, our ability to draw Ministers from those seats will become greater.

Second, our Civil Service will need to further develop its professional, impartial non-political abilities to support and advise the Ministers of parliamentary governments. Parliamentary governments mean that Ministers appointed to a particular portfolio may not have had previous experience in that field. It is vital that the civil service be the repository of highly professional technical advice and that Ministers ask for and act upon the expert opinion and advice provided by the Civil Service.

The third condition is a change in Parliamentary conventions, the way Parliament works, to support parliamentary government. Parliament will be able to begin to develop these conventions after this election and can build them further over time. Ultimately, these conventions will guide the formation of Governments through consultation and consensus among parliamentary blocs. This will require a shared understanding of how such blocs can agree on common policy platforms as a basis for cooperation and stable Government. Opposition parties will similarly need to agree on conventions for how they cooperate in holding the Government to account and offer an alternative vision – their role is just as crucial for successful Government.

Looking ahead: Roles and Responsibilities The more quickly and completely these conditions are fulfilled, the more successful our transition to parliamentary government can and will be. As we make that transition, it will be important that different groups and institutions in our political society take on new and changing roles and responsibilities. In my next paper, I will describe what I believe are the roles and responsibilities of different actors in our system, and make some proposals as to how they should change in the coming years.

3. Each Playing Our Part in a New Democracy By Abdullah II ibn Al Hussein 02 March 2013 The transition to parliamentary government, like democracy itself, is always work in progress. Stakeholders at every level must constantly be aware of their role in shaping the future. In this third discussion paper* on Jordan's political evolution, I would like to focus on our collective way forward, after the landmark parliamentary elections of 23 January 2013. These elections had double significance: They were important per se, and marked a milestone on Jordan's reform path. The democratic and transparent environment in which these elections were held earned them unprecedented national, Arab, and international praise. Voter registration reached 70 percent, and the almost 57 percent turnout was one of highest in our history and internationally. Such participation compares favorably with recent Arab elections, approaching the 62 percent turnouts in Egypt and Libya, and significantly higher than Morocco's 45 percent (a result which itself deservedly won international praise).

Another noteworthy feature in Jordan was urban participation, which increased by approximately 30 percent in Amman and Zarqa. The importance of our election was reflected in the record number of candidates. Eighty percent of political parties participated. First-time Members of Parliament (MPs) make up 61 percent of the new Parliament, showing that the country is more than capable of political renewal. These polls – overseen for the first time by an independent electoral commission, and monitored by international and local observers – brought about a much more representative Parliament. There are blocs from across the spectrum, representing nationalist, Islamist, and leftist parties, as well as popular movements' leaders and activists. The election of eighteen women is a source of special pride: Three women won as leaders of national tickets and local district representatives, in addition to the 15 women who sit in the new Parliament under the women's quota. We shall continue to build on this experience, develop and enhance it. All Jordanians can, and I hope will, contribute, through their continuous, active and responsible participation. But to be effective, parliamentary government will also require properly functioning national political parties with strong platforms, based on a solid framework of national democratic values, enrooted as a democratic culture not just in our institutions but also in our political life. The challenge ahead, for all elements of our political system and all Jordanians, is to deepen this culture. The values needed for a successful democratic transition to parliamentary government are long familiar to Jordanians. Among the most essential are pluralism, tolerance, the rule of law, separation of powers, protection of the inalienable rights of every citizen and group, and guaranteeing that every shade of political opinion gets a fair chance to compete at the ballot boxes. All these guarantees are essential to ensure that at each stage of our country's evolution, both the will of the majority and the rights of all can be secured. In this context, it is essential that we keep developing our electoral system, through our constitutional institutions, so that it becomes fairer and more representative, nurtures pluralism, provides a level playing field, and is conducive to the formation of party-based parliamentary governments. In various international parliamentary government practices, the Prime Minister-designate and Cabinet team may emanate from Parliament or not, or the Cabinet may be a mix of MPs and technocrats. General political practice in parliamentary governments worldwide allows for MPs to serve as ministers, and so does our Constitution, but in parallel with a set of fundamental requirements:

- The first is an advanced set of checks-and-balances that preserves the separation of powers and stipulates monitoring tools.
- The second is the gradual inclusion of MPs in the Cabinet in parallel to the evolvement of politicalparliamentary and political parties work, reflected in the institutionalization and development of parliamentary blocs, whereby they become increasingly platform-based and solid, and eventually party-based. The timeline for this will depend on our

ability to develop effective national parties based on platforms. The transition to parliamentary government will deepen as parliamentary and political parties' work matures over coming parliamentary cycles, reaching a stage in which political parties compete in elections on the basis of their platforms, and independents are also allowed to compete. This will ultimately lead to the emergence, on the one hand, of a parliamentary coalition on party basis that enjoys House majority and forms governments, and, on the other hand, of an opposition parliamentary coalition that serves as "shadow government."

- The third is to develop Civil Service's work so that it becomes more professional, neutral and apolitical, so that it serves as a trusted reference and source of technical support for parliamentary government ministers in their decision-making. The on-going national debate provides a constructive democratic framework to deepen our parliamentary government experience and develop the mechanism for consultations on the selection of the next Prime Minister and whether to include MPs in government and in what percentage.

I. The Role of Political Parties:

Democracy is not just about individuals expressing opinions and points of view. It is about aggregating what individuals say into a set of concrete proposals for joint action that will move the country forward. This is the key role of political parties. In recent years, I have outlined on many occasions my vision for our political system: A small number of major, nationally based political parties, representing views across the spectrum. Only such a system is capable of offering the competition of ideas Jordan needs, as well as achieving the necessary parliamentary consensus on actions to be taken. The focus in the future should be on how to promote national political parties so that voters vote for party-based candidates. In this respect, Jordan's political parties have a challenge and a responsibility:

To help develop and sustain a national perspective in political life.

The national lists in this election were an attempt in this process, one we can assess and learn from as we go forward. We can also learn from other nations' experiences in accelerating political parties' growth. But we must appreciate that political maturity comes from experience, guided by the will of the people through the ballot box.

To work together around shared principles and policy priorities.

I encourage all parties, groups and independents represented in this Parliament to come together around common policy concerns and viewpoints. Creating larger parliamentary blocs can contribute to both parliamentary effectiveness and political development.

To champion clear party platforms and a professional party process.

A fragmented system of weak parties will not earn the trust or engagement of the Jordanian people. To overcome existing public scepticism, political parties will need robust policy platforms that respond to voters' hopes and concerns. Parties need to run professional campaigns aimed at articulating their policies to the nation, winning elections, and forming governments.

II. The Role of Parliament and Parliamentarians:

It is the solemn duty of Parliament to enact legislation in the best interest of the country, and also to hold the Government to account for its decisions. Parliament, in turn, is accountable to the citizens who elected its members. This is the basis for the important responsibilities each MP must fulfil:

To serve as an honest public servant.

In this matter, there can be no compromise: MPs must act in the public interest at all times. Those who serve personal or private interests, or who act on the basis of short-term or populist considerations that are not in the nation's long-term interests, fail the people who elected them and all Jordanians. This is a dereliction of duty, and at its worst, a form of corruption.

To balance local and national interests.

MPs represent the needs of local constituencies, yet must also work together to advance the interests of the Kingdom as a whole. Achieving this balance is one of the most challenging tasks of any MP – but it is the task and the honour of anyone who accepts elected office. MPs best fulfil their dual role through sustainable, broad-interest solutions. Far more constituents can be served, far better and for far longer, when an MP endorses and contributes to policies and programmes that alleviate unemployment and poverty, and acts vigorously and transparently to create local development and jobs, rather than when an MP pressures a government official to give some constituents a public job.

To balance the need for collaboration with the need for constructive opposition.

Striking this balance is the art of effective politics. Parliamentarians must work with each other and with the government to make progress in addressing national challenges. This need to collaborate recognises the fact that MPs are members of one body, Parliament, with a duty to perform; and that the government, too, has a mandate to implement its programme. This reflects the principle of separation of powers, and prevents the encroachment of one branch of government over the other. At the same time, MPs can and must hold the government to account, by constructively challenging proposals and suggesting alternatives, rather than theorising or over- diagnosing the challenges we face instead of suggesting solutions to take us forward within available and sustainable means. This is an invaluable and necessary part of our democracy. It must never be abused as a tool to pursue narrow individual interests or character assassination, or to block proposals simply in order to undermine political opponents. The right balance between collaboration and constructive opposition will determine the effectiveness of future Parliaments.

To work with the government on the basis of objectivity, not opportunism.

To fulfil their public duties, the two branches of government must have a working relationship that is free of pressure and appeasement. The focus must be on the public interest alone. This is essential in the consultation process that leads to the designation of the Prime Minister, the formation of the Cabinet, and its programme. To ensure that this and other processes are not held hostage to pressure, appeasement, and favouritism, parliamentary blocs and political parties have a major monitoring role. In the days ahead, I encourage all MPs and parliamentary blocs to work with determination to develop a parliamentary code of conduct, and internal bylaws of Parliament that will enshrine these responsibilities and translate them into practice.

III. The Role of the Prime Minister and Council of Ministers:

It is the responsibility of the government, led by the Prime Minister and Council of Ministers, to formulate and implement a comprehensive programme of action to enhance the prosperity and security of all Jordanians. The government must present its four-year programme to Parliament and is then held accountable for its implementation. As we move into a new era of parliamentary government, the role of Prime Minister, as well as the skills and attributes required for the post, will evolve. In addition to leading a team of highly competent Ministers and mobilizing the resources of the Civil Service to implement the government's programme in a transparent, timely and efficient manner, the Prime Minister must also interact effectively with a wide range of stakeholders, most importantly the Parliament. Responsibilities that are essential today will become even more vital:

To earn and maintain the confidence of Parliament.

Parliament supports the government by enacting legislation to authorize its actions, and, on behalf of all citizens, holds government to account. Prime Ministers and Cabinets must thus secure and maintain the confidence of Parliament – not just upon their appointment but throughout their tenure. On an on-going basis, they must secure Parliament's support for the legislation required to implement the government programme. This is a complex task, and will require Prime Ministers with the highest integrity, leadership and management skills.

To set standards of excellence for government.

Our people depend on and rightfully demand that their ministers and public servants act efficiently, respectfully, and with dedication. The Prime Minister will be called upon to lead according to best practices. This demands skills and experience in forward planning, policymaking and the Civil Service, excellent communication, negotiation and coalition-building skills, and the ability to build consensus to deal with the challenges facing our citizens.

To champion transparency and good governance, in words and deeds.

In a parliamentary government system, open, transparent and pro-active communication by the Prime Minister and the Council of Ministers with Parliament and with citizens, in addition to ensuring commitment to field-work, will be essential to the success of government.

IV. The Role of the Monarch:

A key part of our political evolution is the development of the role of the Hashemite Constitutional Monarchy. The Hashemite Monarchy has never and will never lose sight of its paramount objective – to safeguard Jordan's prosperity, stability, security, and unity, and ensure the wellbeing of Jordanians. At the same time, the Hashemite Monarchy has constantly evolved with the times and people's aspirations. As our democracy evolves and achieves the milestones I have put forward, it is both inevitable and desirable for the role of the Monarchy to evolve. Let me start by outlining the monarchy's core responsibilities that remain critical for our nation:

The Hashemite Monarchy will remain forward-looking and as monarch I will maintain my role as a unifying leader to prevent polarisation in our society and to protect Jordanian values. The Monarchy will always remain the voice of all Jordanians, and especially the poor and the marginalised. The Monarchy will safeguard our national integrity and justice systems, through continuous improvement and constant diligence, and will continue to promote confidence in Jordanian excellence by championing creativity, recognising success stories, and honouring individual effort and achievement.

As Head of State and Commander-in-Chief of our Armed Forces, I will safeguard paramount issues of foreign policy and national security, acting through the Council of Ministers, which has the Constitutional responsibility to administer state affairs. My role as monarch must ensure that the army, security forces, the judiciary and public religious authorities remain neutral, independent, professional, and unpoliticised as we move along our journey towards a stronger democracy and party-based parliamentary government.

It is equally the Monarchy's responsibility to protect and sustain Jordan's social fabric and religious heritage.

As outlined in my speech to national public figures on 23 October last year, this is a proud and solemn Hashemite duty on behalf of all Jordanians. I have the responsibility and honour of guaranteeing that nothing undermines the fundamental elements that make Jordan unique, special, and an oasis of stability: National unity, pluralism, openness, tolerance and moderation. As a sign of the evolution of the Monarchy's role, my constitutional responsibilities have already begun to change, with the recent constitutional amendments establishing new parameters for the monarch's powers. These amendments enhanced our democracy and enabled citizens to participate more effectively. The Monarchy's role in the formation of governments will continue to evolve in tandem with our maturing parliamentary system. Elements of this maturity, discussed in this and the previous discussion paper, include: Functioning, professional political parties that produce qualified and experienced candidates; party platforms that articulate policies and programmes that voters can weigh; and working processes and structures for parliamentary decision-making, including evidence-based policy proposals from the Civil Service, and active citizen participation. In short, we must act collectively to achieve the reform milestones that lie ahead. I will continue to do my part to enhance political maturity and encourage participation within our society, by remaining the guarantor of our comprehensive reform efforts, championing constructive dialogue among citizens, and safeguarding our stability, security and achievements. My vision for the evolution of the Monarchy is self-motivated and unwavering. I have been reflecting on this vision, on the record, since the early years of my constitutional responsibilities. It is an inclusive vision that does not side with any political group. It is a vision that sides with Jordan and all Jordanians. The Monarchy's progressive role that I envision began with sincere efforts for comprehensive reforms, on parallel tracks, including socio- economic initiatives to empower and expand the middle class – the main driver of political reform. The Arab Spring and its Jordanian dynamics opened new horizons and allowed us to usher in a new wave of reforms and to embark on an irreversible renaissance. It is a future I embrace; one in which all our people will have a voice; one in which no one is excluded from prosperity, security and success.

V. The Role of the Citizen: The final element I wish to discuss is the role of the citizen – the ultimate foundation of our democratic system. Citizen engagement is key to developing the properly functioning political parties we need. Citizens also have the ultimate say in holding government accountable, through their votes, their awareness, and their participation. Fulfilling these vital responsibilities rests on the four core principles for democratic engagement outlined in my first discussion paper: Respect for all fellow citizens, not just those we know or agree with; accountability to one another; honest, constructive dialogue; and sincere compromise.

Voting in elections is one part of this role. I commend all Jordanians who exercised their democratic rights and made their voice heard in the recent election. But while voting is vital, it is not nearly enough in itself. Holding our government and Parliament accountable requires action by citizens each and every day. Three areas of activity are central:

Awareness and search for the truth. Citizens must take the responsibility to become informed about key national issues, based on facts not rumours, and to act on their knowledge.

Generating ideas and solutions. If the government is not considering the best ideas to address the challenges we face, then it is citizens' responsibility to bring those ideas into the public sphere for deliberation and consideration. This simple action can have a huge impact on the future of our country.

Active citizenship. If elected representatives and the government are not fulfilling their commitments, engaged citizens must pressure them to do so. This can be done through community groups, town-hall meetings, or online, through social media and other channels. Responsible, active citizenship creates a public sphere in which dialogue can be the first resort and protests the last resort, all of which are rights guaranteed by our constitution. This is the first step to mutual respect and practical solutions.

The Future: The January elections were a major step, but not the end of our journey. With the elections now behind us, I look forward to working together with successive governments, Parliaments, civil society institutions, and with you – the citizens– to improve the well-being and opportunities of all Jordanians. The change of the modus operandi of the Lower House and the government, in line with what I envisioned in this paper, and the recent Speech from the Throne, will play a key role in our path of democratisation and comprehensive reform as we seek parliamentary and governmental stability, so that Parliament and government can carry out their work in a constructive atmosphere over a full four-year term, as long as the government maintains the confidence of the Lower House, and the Lower House maintains the confidence of the people.

4. Towards Democratic Empowerment and Active Citizenship

By Abdullah II ibn Al Hussein 02 June 2013 Some have argued in the West, and even within our communities, that the Arab world is not interested in or suited for modern politics. They have claimed that democracy is not something the Arab world wants or can handle, and that we are not ready. In Jordan, we have never accepted this view and never will. The renewal of political life across many Arab countries can succeed in meeting the aspirations of Arab people towards a better future, but there are, of course, challenges along this path. As I have said before, this path has not been, and will not always be, smooth and straightforward, but it is inevitable for societies seeking evolution. In Jordan, we are developing a uniquely Jordanian model of democracy, which reflects our distinct culture, aspirations and needs. The previous three discussion papers I wrote came as a contribution to enrich our national dialogue on the model of democracy we seek, its goals, the roles of all stakeholders in the political process, and the milestones we need to achieve to realise this model.

The ideas I suggested highlighted the guarantees that are needed for the success of advancing our democratic transformation, chief among which are: Preserving pluralism, gradualism in evolution, and equality in political opportunities. The course of the journey is now clearer to many sectors of society, who began to vividly recognise that the essential reform goal is to enhance citizens' participation in decision making, by deepening our approach to parliamentary government through successive parliamentary cycles, in order to reach a state where political parties are able to achieve an effective presence in the Lower House of Parliament. This will allow the parliamentary majority to form a party-based and platform-based government, paralleled by a parliamentary minority that works as a shadow government and competes constructively with the ruling majority by providing alternative platforms and policies.

These national parties will compete at the ballot box for the rotation of governments. But one of the key requirements for democratisation efforts is enhancing the role of civil society in monitoring and elevating the political performance of all institutions, by enrooting a democratic culture across society. This is the essence of this fourth discussion paper, which marks the launch of an additional civil society effort geared towards enhancing our democratic model by going grassroots to lay the building blocks for a democratic culture that guarantees a tangible bottom-up change. Consequently, and due to the vital role that civil society plays in enhancing our democratic model, I directed the King Abdullah II Fund for Development to establish a Democracy Empowerment Program (Demoqrati) during my speech on December 10, 2012, on the occasion thof the University of Jordan's 50 anniversary. The official launch of this programme today proves that the realisation of our democratic model will be determined by achieving specific milestones that represent real progress and political maturity, not arbitrary or predefined deadlines. We have already achieved much to be proud of, but ours will be a long and evolutionary journey. Through the twists and turns of our political development, it is our shared commitment to, and confidence in the underlying processes of democracy that will bring us success. This shared commitment and participation is the essence of what I have been referring to in my previous discussion papers as "active citizenship", which I also regard in this paper as an essential condition for democratisation.

Political Participation and Active Citizenship:

Before outlining the mission and goals of Demoqrati, let me first offer my thoughts on the importance of politics and active citizenship. What do I mean when I talk about politics? I mean it in the broadest sense – the process through which we discuss the issues facing our society, argue with mutual respect about our disagreements, and reach workable solutions through constructive debate and compromise. It is an essential means to resolve our differences for the benefit of society as a whole. Politics is also not just about national issues debated under the dome of our Parliament. It is as much about local community issues impacting the daily life of every citizen. Parents concerned about the quality of education at their local school. Commuters concerned about public transport. Neighbours concerned about public services. But politics only works if we all embrace the principle of "active citizenship", which is based on three pillars: The right to participate;

the duty to participate; and the responsibility to participate peacefully and respectfully, and they go hand in hand with the following principles: First, all citizens have the right to engage in political life. The space to freely express divergent political views must be protected. Second, in its essence, politics is a responsibility and a duty. Each citizen must share a part of the burden of deciding on the future we want to build for our children. Our duty as citizens does not end with the act of voting in national elections. That's why it is so important that every Jordanian honours this duty by actively participating in civic and political life on a daily basis. This could be as simple as campaigning on the issues that matter to us, volunteering for civic activities, or joining a political party. Of course, true democracy also means that some can exercise their choice to remain apolitical and disengaged or boycott the political process. But those who take this path are giving up a profound opportunity – and indeed their duty – to contribute to the wellbeing of their country. As citizens, we share a common destiny and therefore a common duty. A mindset of apathy, complacency and mediocrity is the surest way to hold back our development as a nation. We cannot build a better, stronger Jordan without embracing the principle that active citizenship is a duty that must be shouldered by each and every one of us as citizens. Third, active participation in political life also brings with it certain personal responsibilities about how to engage. In my first discussion paper, I outlined four key practices all citizens need to embrace for political life to flourish: Showing respect, engaging actively, embracing dialogue and compromise while rejecting violence, and acknowledging that gains and sacrifices need to be shared.

Moving Forward: Providing Jordanians with the Tools for Active Citizenship:

The official launch today of Demoqrati, the Democracy Empowerment Programme, by the King Abdullah II Fund for Development, marks another milestone along the path of our democratic development journey. Today will be a celebration of all the passion and commitment that many Jordanians, young and old, have already shown in developing our civic and political life. This includes all of you who turned out to vote in this year's elections; all of you who have participated in peaceful constructive rallies for the public interest; and all of you who have led or participated in community activities, whether helping to organise a local boy scouts group, hosting debates and online discussions about current political issues, or others. Demoqrati is set to enroot 'active citizenship' by empowering individuals and organisations with practical ideas about developing our democratic model with some support to do so. By supporting 'social entrepreneurs' to have a greater say in public affairs, Demoqrati will help expand the tools and platforms –debate forums, training programmes and others – available to all Jordanians to enable them to be active and engaged citizens. Demoqrati will initially focus on efforts to increase transparency, provide new ways for Jordanians to discuss and debate critical issues facing the country, and seek to harness the talents and creativity of all Jordanians in the service of society. Jordan already has many examples of organisations actively involved in these and other aspects of our civic and political life.

I commend all of you already working diligently to build civil society across our country for your pioneering efforts. To those who are already doing this important work, Demoqrati will offer the opportunity to gain additional support to expand your activities.

5. Goals, Achievements and Conventions: Pillars for Deepening Our Democratic Transition By Abdullah II ibn Al Hussein 13 October 2014 Almost two years ago, I started contributing to the national debate on reforms in the Kingdom through a series of discussion papers. In the first four papers, I outlined our vision for reform with an end-goal of building a vibrant Jordanian democracy founded on three pillars: a gradual deepening of **parliamentary government**, under the umbrella of our **Constitutional Monarchy**, underpinned by active public participation or what I called "**active citizenship**". Jordan remains resilient in the face of unprecedented regional volatility that surrounds us and the strain it is causing our economy. Despite these challenges, our political reform process has continued, and it is worth reflecting on what has been achieved towards our**goal** of a vibrant Jordanian democracy since my last discussion paper in June 2013. Jordan has succeeded in creating its own spring by genuinely embracing the opportunity to speed up existing political reform efforts based on a gradual, inclusive and evolutionary reform model. Let us also remember that the goal for Jordan's home-grown reform is clear: Empowering people to take the widest role in decision-making through their elected representatives. Deepening our democracy, therefore, translates into deepening our experience of parliamentary governments under our Constitutional Monarchy, reaching an advanced stage where a party-based majority bloc or coalition of blocs forms a government and the remaining minority serves as a shadow government, which would monitor, hold governments to account, offer competing programmes and guarantee democratic rotation of governments. Deepening our democratic transformation requires the right conditions while moving along interconnected parallel tracks. Our approach has been focused on achieving certain milestones. Through this fifth discussion paper,*

I aim to take stock of the milestones we have already achieved on three parallel tracks. I will also discuss the milestones ahead, particularly the values, practices, roles and conventions that need to continue to evolve in order to sustain the momentum of our reform model and reach our end-goal successfully in a manner that is responsive to our citizens.

1. Legislative Milestones: The first track has involved reforming the legislation that represents the skeleton of any democratic system:

A revised Constitution has been endorsed, thereby strengthening the separation of powers through additional checks and balances, enhancing freedoms and generating new democratic institutions. Parliament will soon complete amending over 16 key laws to ensure their compatibility with the revised Constitution.

A package of new political laws has been passed for the first election cycle after the constitutional revision – including laws related to elections, political parties and public gatherings. Together, these laws help foster political society and party formation across the political spectrum.

A new State Security Court Law has been enacted that limits the Court's jurisdiction to treason, espionage, terrorism, drugs and currency counterfeiting and ensures that civilians stand trial only in front of a civilian court.

Finally, the House of Representatives has made important progress in reforming its internal **by-laws** to help improve its operations and effectiveness.

2. Institutional Milestones: His second track has involved strengthening existing and building new democratic institutions:

A Constitutional Court is now in place that specialises in interpreting the Constitution and overseeing the constitutionality of laws and regulations in force and to guarantee that the rights of all Jordanian citizens are upheld in accordance with the Constitution.

An Independent Elections Commission (IEC) has been established and has won recognition in Jordan and internationally for its role in administering parliamentary elections and ensuring transparency through supervising both the parliamentary and municipal elections. Holding these two sets of elections, within the span of only one year, demonstrated confidence and prospects for political renewal. Building on the IEC's success, we recently witnessed the endorsement of further constitutional amendments governing its mandate to include expanding it to administer municipal elections and any other elections such as local governorate councils.

The House of Representatives has recently established a legislative **research centre** to support the work of MPs and specialised parliamentary committees, ensuring that their work and decisions are informed by facts and evidence. And in an effort to enhance **transparency**, the House's Financial Committee held detailed discussions over the 2014 budgets for the Armed Forces, security agencies and the Royal Court. This precedent was initiated by Parliament to develop its oversight mechanisms.

Work is underway to strengthen our **Judiciary** and enhance the **national system for integrity, transparency and accountability**, building on the work of the Royal Committee for Strengthening the National Integrity System, the Privatisation Review Committee, a strong independent Judiciary and a number of key oversight institutions, such as the anti-corruption commission, Audit Bureau, Ombudsman as well as other oversight systems across government, private and civil society sectors.

Work is also underway to support the **National Centre for Human Rights** (NCHR), along with a related network of institutions, so that we strengthen our human rights system and ensure government's follow-up on the recommendations by the NHCR and finalise the National Human Rights Plan.

Continue working on all **public sector reform** paths, through building on achievements in merging institutions within the restructuring plan; in addition to continue developing government services, human resources and decision-making mechanisms.

Finally, and consistent with our evolution towards a fully developed system of parliamentary government, important reforms are underway among our national security agencies. The process started back in 2011 when I publicly entrusted the Director of Intelligence Department with the task of reforming this vital national security body. Most significantly, the government is in the process of strengthening the role of the Ministry of Defense, which will be responsible for all non-combat defense matters and operations as part of government under parliamentary oversight.

3. Milestones of Actors in Our Political System:

The third track has involved identifying values and practices at the heart of a genuine culture of democracy and citizen participation, coupled with roles of key democratic stakeholders, all of which requires their continuous development:

The values needed for successful democratic transition to parliamentary governments

are now familiar to Jordanians and must be enrooted into our culture and society. These values include moderation, tolerance, openness, pluralism, inclusiveness, respect and concern for others, respecting the rule of law and protecting the inalienable rights of every citizen and guaranteeing that participating political platforms get an equal chance to compete at the ballot boxes.

Our 'Jordanian Spring' must also continue to adopt the following **essential democratic practices**:

demonstrating respect for and embracing dialogue, even in the face of disagreement; accepting the reciprocity of rights and responsibilities as citizens; accepting that shared sacrifices lead to shared gains; turning disagreement into finding compromise, while maintaining constant dialogue; and active and constructive participation by all citizens. Stakeholders in our political system – the Monarchy, MPs, government, political parties and citizens – must internalise and apply these values and practices in playing their national roles and exercising their responsibilities. These roles and responsibilities represent a major component of the third reform track:

The Hashemite Monarchy

has the responsibility of providing unifying leadership for all Jordanians and remaining forward- looking to ensure the prosperity not just of the current generation, but of future generations as well. As Head of State and Commander-in-Chief of the Armed Forces, the King is responsible for paramount issues of foreign policy and national security, and for protecting Jordan's social fabric and religious heritage, acting through the Council of Ministers, which has the Constitutional responsibility to administer state affairs. The Monarchy is also the guarantor of the Constitution and the safeguard of neutrality, stability and justice, which intervenes to break deadlocks between parliaments and governments when they arise.

Members of Parliament

have the responsibility of serving as honest public servants, who balance local and national interests and match the need for collaboration with government to the need to serve the role of constructive opposition. They are responsible for working with the government on the basis of objectivity, not opportunism, and for maintaining Parliament as a genuine forum of national democratic dialogue.

Government, embodied in the Prime Minister, Ministers and Civil Servants,

Is responsible for developing and executing comprehensive programmes for improving the economic opportunities and social well-being Jordanians deserve and aspire for. In doing so, it must earn and maintain the confidence of Parliament according to its policy plan, set standards of excellence for government performance, and champion transparency, good governance and partnership with the private sector and civil society in words and deeds.

Political parties have a responsibility to form into a small numbe of major nationally-based parties, representing views across the spectrum and to champion clear party platforms.

Citizens have the responsibility to participate actively and constructively in all aspects of political life. I am delighted to see that more and more Jordanians embracing the spirit of 'active citizenship' at the national and local levels that I called for last year. Over the last five years, our civil society organisations have doubled in number, reaching over 6,000 active organisations. We want these organisations to continue to strengthen their capacity to address citizens' concerns, inform policy making and act as national watchdogs. I am particularly excited to see that over 1,000 concept notes have been submitted in the first two rounds of the Youth Empowerment Window, established by **Demoqrati**, a democratisation and youth empowerment initiative launched in June last year under King Abdullah II Fund for Development. This includes young Jordanians like Furat Malkawi, who established a model student parliament in her school in Arjan, based on democratic principles and standards, introducing concepts of platforms, campaigning, ethical code of conduct and safeguards for clean elections. *Demoqrati* also supported Hannieh Dmour, who produced 12 interactive episodes of a debate programme for local community radio in Karak, encouraging a more positive action-oriented attitude towards local issues, in addition to Mohammad Alumour, whose initiative addresses student violence on campuses through debate sessions and theater as well as training on negotiation, communications and conflict-management skills in universities. This is active citizenship. Demoqrati will shortly launch an equally important new initiative, Akeed, in partnership with the Jordan Media Institute. By helping to check and verify news reports concerning government and elected politicians in popular media outlets from newspapers to websites, Akeed is designed to help citizens become fully and accurately informed about issues that matter to them - an important new element of making our political system more transparent and accountable to the public.

Looking Ahead: As I look ahead to the next set of milestones we must set out to achieve, it is important that each of the actors in our political system work hard to fulfill their role and execute their responsibilities with a high standard of excellence and integrity. While we have made significant progress in recent years, we still have a lot more to accomplish:

Lawmakers must improve **key political laws**, assuring consensus and enhancing our parliamentary government experience. Priority should be given to local governance through finalising municipal elections and decentralisation laws first because upcoming municipal and governorates local councils' elections are due in less than two years. Once passed, we move to enact the next generation parliamentary elections law since parliamentary elections are due in less than three years and will depend on the outcome of local governance package. **Parliament** must enhance parliamentary blocs as they encourage political parties and continue developing its conventions including a **code of conduct**.

Governments must continuously develop the **public sector** and the **Civil Service** so that they are highly professional, impartial, non-political and capable of producing evidence-based policy proposals advising future ministers of parliamentary governments. Moreover, governments must devise **long-term government strategies and action plans**, based on effective public consultations, **transparency and accountability** in announcing budgets and managing national projects. Government must also proceed in creating a Ministry of Defense.

Political parties must continue to develop their internal systems and capabilities so that they evolve into well-functioning, professional, platform-based national parties, capable of winning a majority of votes. They must also focus on producing competent leaders who can assume positions in government so as to enable an advanced form of parliamentary government. In parallel, efforts should continue to enhance the performance of parliamentary blocs in the House of Representatives because they can provide impetus towards platform-based national parties.

Efforts must continue to build our Judiciary's capacities, due to its central role in government; in addition to ongoing efforts to build the capacities of the **Constitutional Court** and the **Independent Elections Commission** so that they can realise their full potential and perform according to international best practices and become regional centres of excellence.

The Royal Committee for Evaluating the Progress of the National Integrity System's Executive Plan must continue overseeing the implementation of the National Integrity System's recommendations.

Our **civil society organisations, including universities and think tanks, in addition to the private sector** need to play a greater role in contributing analyses and ideas to the search for solutions to challenges facing the Kingdom. To facilitate that, we must continue investing in research and civil society organisations, scaling up successful initiatives and promoting dialogue, volunteerism, accountability, transparency and the right to access information. One of the major challenges we face during a period of change is preserving the delicate balance between branches of government, so that they continue to work together effectively and remain independent from each other at the same time. Our Constitution and laws facilitate this balance, but democracies around the world and throughout history have shown that it is simply impossible for any constitution or set of laws to anticipate and prepare for every possible situation. Part of the answer to striking this delicate balance between cooperation and separation is in our political actors' ability to make the best decisions in situations that are not clearly covered by stated rules and regulations. This is known as **'Conventions' – a set of habits and practices that govern political actors' conduct**. Conventions play an important role in every system of government around the world, especially in parliamentary systems, as I mentioned briefly in my second discussion paper. Although conventions represent habits and practices that are not written down and may not have the force of law, they are vital for the effective and practical functioning of our political system. An important example of one of our important political conventions is the practice of issuing a letter of designation by the King to Prime Ministers. Through this convention, we are able to identify the key tasks and responsibilities awaiting the government. The letter also provides benchmarks to assess the governments' performance. **Government, Parliament and the Civil Service** must, therefore, develop further the conventions that already exist and build new ones as new changes and challenges arise. Areas in which enhancing existing conventions and building new ones are needed to ensure effective collaboration and coordination between our political actors include:

The **consultative mechanism for designating prime ministers**, as our practices of parliamentary democracy continue to evolve.

The mechanism for **formulating the PM-designate and his Cabinet's four-year policy plan** as part of the basis to receive the House of Representatives' vote of confidence.

Regulating **question-and-answer sessions** from Parliament to government ministers, in a manner that upholds principles of transparency and accountability and the government's right to govern without threatening a no confidence vote or calling for an enquiry whenever MPs are displeased with a decision because it contradicts shortsighted personal or group interests.

Identifying the roles of Ministers, MPs and the Civil Service during government change, handovers and caretaking periods. These include: durations spanning the consultation period needed to designate a new prime minister, the caretaking period needed until a new government is formed and the duration needed until the House of Representatives grants government a vote of confidence based on its ministerial team and its four-year policy plan.

6. Rule of Law and Civil State By Abdullah II ibn Al Hussein 16 October 2016 In my previous five discussion papers, I put forward several ideas and visions related to Jordan's political reform path. These included advancing crucial democratic practices, identifying the roles of stakeholders in the political process and articulating the ultimate end goal for reform efforts – achieving an envisioned level of democratic participation necessary to secure young generations with a promising future of prosperity and stability. Since the last discussion paper, many developments have taken place. Conflicts have deepened and our region is undergoing radical transformations, triggering grave repercussions on regional countries, including our beloved country. It is perhaps not an overstatement to say that no single country in recent history has endured as many external shocks as Jordan has. Despite conflicts and wars surrounding us, disintegration of neighbouring societies, and the influx of refugees seeking the safety and dignity they were denied in their homeland. Despite all odds and challenges, we have proved to ourselves and the entire world – time and again – that we stand tall, strong and resolute in our unity. As I see how generous and giving our country is, I find myself deeply touched by the kindness of Jordanians and so proud of your determination and patriotism. I know that each and every one of you, no matter how your perspectives may differ, will find at least a small place of pride in your hearts for our beloved Jordan. Those of you living abroad will have experienced firsthand the tremendous respect and admiration the world has for our country – with all that it represents and all that it stands for. Today, we are at a critical crossroads surrounded with challenges. We must determine our path carefully, fully aware of the challenges at hand, and chart our way forward towards our future with a clear vision to achieve our ambitions and pass onto generations a legacy of peace, security, prosperity, dignity and the strength to overcome the most difficult challenges.

But for us to remain resilient in the face of present challenges and to progress and prosper into the future, there is one aspect that I would like to focus on today. To me it is the main underpinning of a properly functioning nation. It is the one factor that differentiates between a 'developed' and 'developing' nation. It is the very foundation upon which successful democracies, prosperous economies, and well-functioning societies are built. It is the guarantor of individual and public rights, provider of the framework for effective administration, the architecture for a safe and fair society and the accelerator for growth and prosperity. I am referring, of course, to the rule of law. Respecting rule of law is the one true expression of love for our country. Declarations of loyalty and devotion to Jordan remain abstract and theoretical in the absence of respect to laws. The state is responsible for upholding the rule of law with justice, equality and integrity. On the other hand, citizens are responsible for observing laws in their daily lives.

I say this because experience has taught me that individuals accept and embrace the rule of law in principle, while in practice, some believe they are the "exception" and excused from applying it. Rule of law cannot be applied selectively and it supersedes social status, rank and family connections. I feel so disheartened and outraged when I learn that a young girl has died in the arms of her father because of festive firing in weddings or celebrations, or when a mother loses her son in a car accident because of a reckless driver, or when an excellent student loses an opportunity he has every right to, or when a criminal enjoys freedom without accountability. All of this happens when rule of law is not upheld. These are examples which we all know and can relate to, they touch the essence of our rights and they sow division amongst us.

As I look at the harrowing and saddening state of many of the nations in our region, I see clearly that the absence of rule of law and its fair application was a major factor that contributed to the situation today. Our region is a made up of a complex matrix of diverse religious, racial, ethnic, sectarian and tribal constituents. This diversity can lead to social and cultural enrichment, political pluralism, and economic enhancement or it can foment nationalism, ethnic conflict or even war. The dividing line between these two realities is demarcated by the presence or absence of rule of law. Respect for the rights of minority groups should be viewed as a guarantor for the rights of the majority. If any member of our society feels unsafe or unfairly treated because he or she belongs to a minority, then all of us must feel that we are standing on shaky grounds. All our citizens have inalienable rights that must be safeguarded. The rule of law is the main underwriter of these rights and it is, therefore, the most effective enforcer of social justice. I have great regard to what we are today but have even greater ambitions for what we can become. But not one of my dreams for our nation can be realised in the absence of rule of law.

I see it as the foundation that grounds us, the pillar that holds us and the bridge that can carry us to a better future. And I ask every citizen to show respect for our beloved country by respecting its laws, express love to our country by extolling its laws, show loyalty to our country by never acting above the law, and to pledge that respect for rule of law will be the essence of our individual and collective actions.

Rule of law: the essence of prudent state administration

As I have said, every citizen, official and state institution must fulfil the duty of protecting and enhancing the rule of law, which is the essence of a prudent administration that adopts justice and equality as the pillars of its approach. We cannot achieve sustainable development, empower our creative youth or successfully execute our development plans unless we develop state administration and enhance the rule of law through strengthening the principles of justice, equality and transparency. These noble principles are the basis of the Great Arab Awakening and Revolt and this year we celebrate its centennial anniversary.

Political reform can only yield its fruits when an effective and clear approach for realising the rule of law is in place. Moreover, the positive steps achieved on the path of political reform, starting with the constitutional amendments of 2011 and the ensuing legislation regulating political life namely, elections and decentralisation laws – must be coupled with profound and drastic administrative reforms aimed to enhance the rule of law, advance administration and modernise procedures. These steps should pave the way for administrative leadership capable of delivering and leading change so that a new and competent echelon can take over administrative posts, equipped with the needed vision and abilities to serve citizens with dedication. Here, it is worth noting the efforts of the government and various institutions seeking to ensure a prudent administration of the state. Indeed, there have been national and inclusive endeavours towards this goal, namely the formation of the National Integrity Committee, which resulted in the National Integrity Charter and its Executive Plan detailing responsibilities and timeframes.

A Royal Committee was consequently formed and tasked with the follow-up and evaluation of the national integrity system, it recommended establishing a new Integrity and Anti-Corruption Commission, incorporating under its umbrella the previous Anti-Corruption Commission and Ombudsman Bureau, in an effort to streamline and boost efforts as well as advance transparency and justice. Rule of law is meant to ensure that principles of justice, equality, transparency and accountability are upheld by all state institutions and community members, with no exception, especially officials in leading positions. This needs to be translated into practices on the ground as there is not a single administration that can continue with its reform efforts and enhance its performance without adopting rule of law as a constant approach and key pillar in its work. Accepting the rule of law is an essential requirement for a successful democratic transformation. No democracy that respects human rights can work outside this framework. Accordingly, all government and other state agencies share accountability for decisions, policies and measures they take. Parliament exercises its legislative and oversight role, while the independent and impartial judiciary and security agencies are tasked with applying the law in a manner that assures citizens that they and their families are protected by laws that are applied with no discrimination. And the law has to be fully applied on officials as it is applied on private citizens. Laws, moreover, should be based on transparent and clear legislation and the law enforcement process should be managed prudently and efficiently. A well-functioning system of accountability has prerequisites, foremost of which is that our institutions adopt binding codes of conduct that govern the work and performance of institutions and authorities. Our national institutions should also formulate a clear vision, action plans and goals. This will allow state institutions to achieve their goals and measure progress and seek the highest standards of integrity and transparency, as well as best quality of services provided to citizens. Ensuring that the rule of law is upheld requires effective oversight mechanisms. These include internal audit units functioning within ministries and institutions, the Audit Bureau and Integrity and Anti-Corruption Commission, along with Parliament, which has a constitutional oversight role. These units and institutions should put the interests of the country and citizens first and foremost, while the judiciary looks into appeals and complaints against administrative decisions and corruption cases.

Wasta and nepotism

We cannot address the issue of rule of law without recognising that wasta and nepotism jeopardise development efforts. Wasta does not only impede the country's progression, it erodes achievements by undermining the values of justice, equal opportunity and good citizenship, which are the enablers of development in any society. We cannot tolerate such practices that destroy the bases of public service. We cannot allow them to become a source of frustration for our qualified youth, by leaving our young generations victim to the conviction that their future, whether in college or in the job market, hinges on their ability to benefit from wasta and nepotism. How can a generation brainwashed with sub-loyalties assume the responsibilities of protecting rule of law or running national institutions? This challenge warrants a comprehensive national strategy on youth, devising programmes designed by experts and prominent institutions with the aim of cementing values of good citizenship, the state of law and love of the country. These programmes should also empower young people to realise their potential and expand their horizons and immune them against extremist evil ideologies. Senior government appointments surface as a topic and dominate the conversation, whenever wasta and nepotism are addressed. We have, regrettably, seen in recent years some transgressions that burdened our institutions and citizens with unqualified officials. These practices have deprived institutions from qualified personnel and leadership that can advance these agencies and serve the country and the people. It should be emphasised here that meritocracy should be the only basis for appointment.

Advancing the judiciary and enhancing rule of law

Rule of law cannot be upheld unless a qualified, impartial and efficient judicial apparatus is in place. Citizens resort to the judiciary because they have confidence in its ability to deliver them justice and safeguard their rights as swiftly as possible. If we lose that, people's confidence in the judicial system will be shaken. Jordan has always been renowned for its qualified judicial apparatus. We often pay tribute to judges who are well remembered and revered for their contributions to the advancement of our well respected judiciary. However, litigation can often be lengthy and there is a shortage in personnel and in certain judicial specialties. These challenges, inter alia, adversely affect the performance of the apparatus and the rights of citizens and investors.

Rule of law: the sine qua non of civil state

The term "civil state" has been actively debated recently. Some even contested the concept, which seems to be the result of confusion and lack of understanding of what it really stands for. A civil state is one that is governed by a constitution and laws that apply to all citizens without exception. It is a state of institutions that guarantee separation of powers through a system of checks and balances, preventing any power from encroaching on the other. It is a state built on peace, tolerance and harmony and is distinguished for respecting and safeguarding pluralism, respecting different opinions and protecting all members of the community, regardless of their religious or intellectual affiliation. It is a state that protects rights and guarantees freedoms, where all are equal in their rights and obligations. It is a state to which citizens resort when their rights are violated. It guarantees religious freedom for its citizens and enroots tolerance and respect of others in society. It protects the rights of women and minorities. These principles constitute the essence of a civil state. This is not synonymous with a secular state. In a civil state, religion is a key contributor to the value system and social norms. Religion is also enshrined in our constitution. However, we will not allow anyone to manipulate religion to serve political interests or gains for a specific faction. In the conducts of Prophet Mohammad, peace be upon him, we find a great inspiring example in the Medina Charter after he migrated from Mecca to Medina, with the aim of regulating the relationship between all sects and groups in the city, including Muslims from Mecca (muhajirin) and Medina (ansar) as well as Jews. Many observers consider such a pact a unique and early civil charter in history that is a landmark achievement for the Islamic state and a milestone in its political legacy. It was based on the principle of citizenship in terms of rights and obligations and placed them all under the protection of the state in return for defending it. In summary, the civil state is one that upholds rule of law and is governed by a constitution and laws. It is a state that endorses active citizenship, pluralism and difference in opinions. It is a state where citizens have equal rights and duties, without any discrimination based on religion, language, color, gender, race, class, political affiliation or intellectual views.

7. Developing Human Resources and Education Imperative for Jordan's Progress

By Abdullah II ibn Al Hussein 15 April 2017 Education has lately been the subject of heated global debate. It has been heartening to see this trend pick up in our part of the world, Jordan in particular. I believe this discussion bodes well, since it signifies a widespread awareness of the importance of this issue, and rightly so, since education is key to nation-building and improving our world, at a time of a global race to realise knowledge economies and invest in human resources. We cannot keep up with the rapid developments of this era without utilising its novel knowledge tools and latest technologies. Within that context, we must comprehensively address the urgent challenges facing our education sector to overcome them effectively and arrive at a modern education system–pivotal to building the future we seek. The implementation of the recommendations of the National Committee for Human Resources Development is an integral part of the process.

Investing in Our Children, Investing in Our Future

Our people are our most valuable asset. Armed with a modern, quality education, Jordanians will become agents of change. To that end, we must ardently invest in education. It is the most rewarding investment, and I firmly believe that every Jordanian is entitled to an opportunity to pursue a good education, excel and realise his or her highest potential. In their pursuit of unlimited knowledge and excellence, Jordanians must remain confident, determined and open to all cultures, embracing shared values. This vision is only attainable if we are united–people, government, and public and private institutions working together to ensure an enabling environment and meet the needs to build capacities through an effective education system that delivers, and is led by men and women from across the Jordanian spectrum.

Our Path to a Prosperous Future Educational institutions must believe in the immense energies, promising capabilities, and diverse talents of our youth. They should seek to cultivate and channel these qualities, driving young men and women to unleash their potential. Therefore, modern teaching methods should be adopted to encourage critical and deductive thinking, rather than rote learning. Moreover, these methods should combine theory and practice, field and classroom, as well as analysis and planning. Such an educational system would widen horizons for our youth, so that they can excel in every art, profession, or craft. We cannot allow fear of change nor reluctance to embrace modernisation and scientific advancement to waste the vast potential of our tremendous human resources. We will not tolerate miring this strategic sector and the future of Jordanians in petty politicking and narrow interests; this is an alarming path, for education must rise above all such issues if we are to continue with our reform and development endeavours to create a better present and future. History stands as testament to the necessity and inevitability of change. Those who tried to oppose it have failed time and time again. Jordanians are known as champions of modernisation and progress in our Arab world, who lean forward and take ownership and initiative.

We are innovators, pioneers and changemakers, proud of our rich Arabic and Islamic heritage, which rejects discord and division. Constantly seeking renewal, we draw inspiration from and reflect on our history to learn from it and create a better tomorrow instead of remaining tied to the past. In this modern, high-tech age, education cannot be reduced to reading and writing; it goes way beyond that to encompass mastering computer and Internet literacy, major international languages, communication skills, professional work ethics, critical thinking and analytical skills. Once they gain these abilities, students will be able to produce knowledge and contribute to progress, heeding the teachings of the Holy Quran: "O my Lord! advance me in knowledge." We have been blessed with a rich language, deep-rooted heritage and noble values. For our students to fully appreciate and experience that heritage, mastering Arabic is a must. It is the language of the Holy Quran and the Ummah's unifying tongue. It shapes their culture and defines their episteme.

Jordan: Beacon of Science and Knowledge

We aspire towards a strong Jordan that arms its children with the finest education to empower them to take on the challenges ahead, launching successful businesses, practising impactful crafts, starting loving families, and building a cohesive society. We seek a Jordan that takes its rightful place among the countries leading educational transformation. Our gate to the future lies in building capacities through quality education and excellent graduates. Education is an effective tool to transcend differences and build common ground to spread tolerance and understanding, and shun bigotry and extremism. There can be no comprehensive reform without an educational transformation. We want Jordan to lead the way in modernising education in the Arab world, encouraging others to follow in its footsteps towards a knowledge-based society. Reforming education is a challenge before us all, and expertise exchange among Arab countries will help us take on this challenge. Our schools, vocational training centres, and universities should graduate great thinkers, talented craftspeople, and productive individuals. Schools should identify students' interests, harness their talents, and build their capacities. Schools should be incubators of change, graduating students after equipping them with the skills to face challenges and build Jordan's bright future. Schools should graduate students who know how to think, how to learn, how to seize opportunities, and how to develop innovative problem-solving skills.

This calls for a modern educational system that expands students' horizons, teases their curiosity, and bolsters their sense of self-worth to assume their role as global citizens rooted in their Arab and Islamic identity, and heritage. For this to come to fruition, it is vital to have curricula that instil critical and analytical thinking, pushing students to ask questions and weigh various opinions, and encouraging them to respect different views by pursuing the culture of dialogue and diversity—all the while guided by capable teachers who are qualified to raise future generations. It is indeed heartening to contribute to this vibrant debate on how best to educate our daughters and sons and to empower our human resources. This decisive issue lies at the core of our nation's future, and a healthy discussion is a sign of awareness that I fully support, and I look forward to seeing it culminate into tangible reforms and outcomes. We must all work together as one students, teachers, parents, and institutions to reach our goal. Every day offers an opportunity for our youth to fulfil their potential; let us seize it and grant them what they deserve.

Conclusion:

The Jordanian state faces many political, economic, and social challenges, a state of social disintegration, shrinking in community roles, a high state of political frustration, inefficient institutions, lack of prestige of the state sometimes, low confidence in institutions in addition to inter economic challenges that affect the lives of citizens, yet, the clarity of our leadership's vision, drives the leadership to strive to emerge out of these challenges or at least restrain them so as not to deteriorate more, as the leadership has a clear vision in the process of comprehensive reform and has an ambitious plan to move the state and the components to state to a modern state with a modern democratic system, based on popularly elected parliamentary governments to embody the principle of the nation as source of authority, and to achieve Justice, Equality, liberty and to expand the base of political participation, and based of the aforementioned.

What is required of all social and political forces is to engage in the political process to achieve the king's ambitious and serious vision to promote Jordan to the ranks of modern states, after amending more than a third of the constitution's articles, and after all democratic process related laws have been amended such as : the electoral law, the law of the independent election Commission, the law of the Constitutional Court, and the law of political parties. And thus the legal structure of democratic life has been completed, and this requires all the political and social components to actively engage in the upcoming political process, And therefore those who wish to make a change through peaceful, legal, and democratic means must work from within the system rather than from the outside.

There is no doubt that the Jordanian situation has been affected by the Arab Spring, which happened in many countries of the region, and that those changes have cast their shadow on the situation, and affected the moral of individuals and had them demand higher ceilings of freedom, which led to situations of loss of control sometimes, but the Jordanian political system and through its institutions interacted with such events in a realistic and practical manner, away from violence or the use of force, in an attempt to absorb and contain the demands and expectations within capabilities, and in the context of realistic political analysis, it is reasonable to say that the Jordan has witnessed two types of popular movements.

First: a political movement demanding the acceleration of the political process and to combat corruption and to promote integrity, rejecting the -one man, one vote - system, and calling for the adoption of the principle of equal proportional representation, and to reducing the constitutional powers of the King, this movement is led by the Islamic movement (the Muslim Brotherhood) and their political hand the Islamic action Front, and some other political forces such as the nationalists and the leftist. This movement rejects the principles of a gradual reform process, and demands the achievement of its demands as a precondition imposed on the system before starting the political process, and wants more compromise from the system before making something tangible or practical, and we believe in engaging in serious dialogue with this movement on the basis of the principle of compromise, "give and take, and by sharing not by beating, and the desire of the system to involve everyone in the political process without the desire to exclude anyone, or to keep anyone alone on the political street, for political pragmatism is required of the leaders of this movement in dealing with the case of Jordan, because the practical and legal foundation that has been set for the path of real reform in the structure of the State, and because the state refuses the principals of extremism or the use of violence that no one wants, and at the same time, what is required from the government is to bridge the gap, and push for dialogue based on the higher national interests.

The second movement: which is a popular movement that calls for services from the state, existing in most areas of Jordan, expanding at times especially at times of crisis, and shrinks back in other times, we believe that this type of movement must be addressed through providing the basic and urgent demands to citizens, services such as water, electricity, and improved wages, and to improve their standard of living, as well as to improve health services and employment, and to address issues of poverty, and so on. The solution in this case is in the hands of government, and the role of governmental institutions who's services have deteriorated especially in recent years, The effectiveness of governments is needed today more than ever, as field work and to meet challenges is inevitable, if we were to combat the core of the problems. Thus, if we want to resolve problems at the core, enabling relevant ministries is the only choice, in order to address all imbalances occurring in many provinces of the country. The restoration of the citizen's confidence in institutions and their role requires extra effort by all those in authority.

One of problems facing the system's structure is the frequent change of ministries and cabinet reshuffles where the average age of a ministry does not exceed nine months, with years having three ministries, and therefore those ministries are ministries that carry trivial tasks and not ministries that can combat and resolve serious issues, and therefore become part of the problem instead of the solution, not to mention the absence of precise criteria for selecting ministers such as ability, efficiency, experience, social background, and the knowledge of the challenges facing the state, where sometimes ministers are appointed and dismissed and one does not know why they are appointed? And how and why they were dismissed? Such problems have increased the level of slack administration and corruption, and lowered the level of achievement and deepened favoritism, mediation, personalization, cronyism, and serving narrow self-serving interests at the expense of serving the country and its interests, and this problem must be addressed in terms of finding a widely accepted exact criteria to finding governments with a higher average life than the current average, allowing for enough time to hold the ministry accountable, and to allow it to be effective and practical in the face of the challenges facing the state, and to be able to develop and implement practical solutions on the ground rather than the useless theorizing.

The decline in prestige of the state with its various institutions is due to several reasons, including the misunderstanding of the concept of freedom, liberties are essential but must be based on the principle of responsibility and respect for public order, while the other reason is due to the weakness of institutions in the face of meeting challenges and demands, and its failure to function and the loss of confidence in it and in its abilities. As well as its inability to find fair and suitable solutions, an important factor in the downturn, in addition to the absence of justice and the absence of the principle of the rule of law, rampant cronyism, nepotism, corruption, and the widespread power of executives, restoring honor of the state requires upholding the principle of the rule of law and to achieve justice wholly, equality and fairness in dealing with social components, where everyone attains his or her rights, not to mention the importance of weakening the role of "centres of power" in the state structure.

While the more urgent problem is that narrow affiliations are on the rise at the expense of the sense of belonging to the state and loyalty to the system, which is a basic requirement for democracy, the weakness of state institutions, and the decline in its prestige, and the weakness of civil society organizations, led to a situation of social and cultural retreat and a return to traditional components such as: tribalism, clan affiliation, and clan affiliation for the purpose of protection from state institutions, the restoration of belonging to the state, and loyalty to the political system requires reconsideration of the prevailing system of social values which in itself is a corner stone of the pillars of political reform, requiring the enabling of the institutions of social and political development such as, family, schools, universities, political parties, the media, religious institutions and others. As for the structure of the political system and its constitutional base, amendments to the constitution led to the loss of balance between powers, as it is known that parliamentary systems are based on the principles of balance between powers, especially the balance between the executive and the legislature.

This principle has been breached by giving more powers to the legislative authority at the expense of the executive, violating the previous principle, for example, unexclusively, the statement that the government that dissolves the House of Representatives must resign a week after the date of dissolution, typically, in parliamentary systems, the government has the right to recommend the dissolution to the king, which is faced by the right of the legislature to withdraw confidence in the government, the two aforementioned rights are opposing laws, and such a principle must not be compromised, for in this case, the legislature has the right to dissolve the government which is responsible for dissolving the parliament, as it is a punishment that will sometimes make the government hesitant to dissolve the parliament, adding to that the prime minister of that resigned government may not be appointed prime minister for the following government, which is a second condition imposing more restrictions on the powers of the king that are mentioned in article 35 of the constitution, and therefore such an amendment contradicts the principle of balance between powers, and must be amended in order to bring things back to normal as it is the case in all parliamentary systems worldwide.

The formation of parliamentary governments requires the presence of political parties, that are able to reach the parliamentary majority through elections that take place on this basis, or a coalition of several political parties to reach the absolute majority (50% +1) to form a coalition government, but in the current state of affairs in Jordan, this is not very feasible, and parliament will resort to a coalition of parliamentary blocs to arrive at a majority, but the problem in the Jordanian case lies in the weakness of the parliamentary blocks' structure, since none of them share an ideology, nor do they share a vision of a clear and precise program, but rather on the basis of personal interest which leads to the quick collapse of such blocks, leading to the dismissal of governments.

As for the Jordanian experience in appointing ministers from the house of representatives, that experiment failed, especially when such appointments were expanded during the years 1996-1997, and therefore, practicing the same methods of that experience requires a better understanding and the adoption of precise criteria, and it is our belief that the situation of Jordan in the formation of future parliamentary governments requires an incremental gradual approach and not to rush in order to prevent falling into the same previous mistakes. And last but not least, the continuation and existence of political systems depends on the degree of political adaptation with demands and expectations, and adaptation to the rapidly changing variables, the more the political system is able to accommodate the demands and expectations, and its ability to handle such demands and expectations in a serious and effective manner, the more it will be able to proceed, and therefore the Jordanian political system adapts gradually with rapid change, and the system of comprehensive reforms is clear evidence of that, but such matters require a more effective performance, and requires speed in delivery, as slow reform hinders the system's abilities of political adaptation, and can lead the system to a critical situation.

Numerical indicators:

The area of the Hashemite Kingdom of Jordan is 89.318 thousand km squared, and has a land area of 88.778 km squared, and a water area "territorial waters of the State" of 540 km squared. Desert areas (the desert) accounts for up to 78.4% of the total area. As for the population, in 2016, the population reached 9.798.000 (Nine million and almost three quarter of a million), and the population growth rate reached 2.2%, and the proportion of people aged below 15 years reached 37.3% and those who are between 15 and 64 years of age accounted for 59.5%. As for the distribution of the population by region, Urban and city dwellers make up 82.6% of the population, while the rural or countryside population reached 17.4%, the population is distributed on twelve governorates, and governorates have populations as follows.

Amman 4,119,500 (42% of the total population), followed by Irbid having a population of 1.819.600 (18.6%), followed by Zarqa 1,403,000 (14.3%), The number of school students is at about one million and six hundred thousand, the number of university students is at 242,000 distributed between 32 public and private universities, and the illiteracy rate in the Kingdom for the population aged 15 years and over is around 6.7%, and an unemployment rate of 18.5% of the total workforce.

While the poverty rate can be up to 14.7% of the total population, measured as being below the poverty line of 504 J.D./Year per capita. The average age (life expectancy) is 73 years, 71.6 for males and 74.4 for females, while the number of families is at 1157020, spending on education from the general budget contributes to 8.5% of the general budget, the budget of the Ministry of Health is up to 6.7% of the general budget, the number of hospitals for the year 2016 reached 106 hospitals and 11.991 thousand beds, and there is 42.3% of the population who are using a personal computer.

Table No.4: Estimated Population by Governorate, Sex and Pop. Density (P/Km2), (2016)

Governorate	Male	Female	Total	% of Total	Pop. Density (P/Km2)
Amman	2211700	1907800	4119500	42.0	543.5
Balqa	271400	234000	505400	5.2	451.7
Zarqa	741800	661200	1403000	14.3	294.7
Madaba	102800	91700	194500	2.0	207.0
Irbid	940200	879400	1819600	18.6	1157.7
Mafraq	291500	273800	565300	5.8	21.3
Jarash	126700	117000	243700	2.5	594.7
Ajlun	93200	87800	181000	1.8	431.3
Karak	170000	155500	325500	3.3	93.1
Tfiela	51800	47200	99000	1.0	44.8
Ma'an	77500	70600	148100	1.5	4.5
Aqaba	109400	84000	193400	2.0	28.0
The Kingdom	5188000	4610000	9798000	100.00	110.4

Table No. 5: Estimated Population of the Kingdom, Area (Km2) and Population Density by Governorate, at the end of 2016

Governorate	Population density	Area		Population
		%	Km2	
Amman	543.5	8.54	7579	4119500
Balqa	451.1	1.26	1120	505400
Zarqa	294.7	5.36	4761	1403000
Madaba	207.0	1.06	940	194500
Irbid	1157.7	1.77	1572	1819600
Mafraq	21.3	29.90	26551	565300
Jarash	594.7	0.46	410	243700
Ajlun	431.3	0.47	420	181000
Karak	93.1	3.94	3495	325500
Tafiela	44.8	2.49	2209	99000
Ma'an	4.5	36.98	32832	148100
Aqaba	28.0	7.78	6905	193400
Total	110.3	100.00	88794	9798000

BIBLIOGRAPHY

A- Laws Charters:

- Amended Electoral Act No. 28 of 2012
- Constitutional Court Act No. 15 of 2012.
- Decentralization Act No. 49 of 2015.
- Election Act No. 25 of 2012
- Election Act No. 34 of 2011.
- Independent Electoral Commission Act No. 11 of 2012.
- Integrity and anti-Corruption Act No. 13 of 2016.
- Jordanian Constitution, E7 with amendments 2011, 2014, and 2016
- Jordanian Constitution, publications of the Council of the Nation, Amman 1986
- Jordanian National Charter, Publications of the Ministry of
- Information, Amman, 1991. ☐ Jordan's amended constitution of 2012, Amman 2012.
- **National Charter and democratization in Jordan**, (1997), Amman: Jordan's New Centre.
- National Pact and democratic transition in Jordan, new Jordan Centre, Amman, 1997.
- Political Parties Act No. 19 of 2007.
- Political Parties law of 2012.
- Rules of procedure of the House of Representatives, publications of the Parliamentary, 1996
- The Basic Law.

- **The Jordanian National Charter**, (1991), Amman: a publication of the Ministry of information.
- The Jordanian Parties Law No. 39 of 2015.

B- The books:

- Abidi, Haydar, (1965), **Jordan: A Political study,** New Delhi: Asia Publishing House.
- Abu Jaber, Kamel (1969). The Jordanian parliament in man, atate and society in contemporary middle east.
- **Accidents magazine**, Issue 2237, September 1999.
- Al Hussien, King Abdullah Ibn, (1950), **The Memoirs of King Abdullah of Jordan**, London: Philosophical Library.
- Al- Mashaqbeh, Amin, (2012), **The King and the three power**, Amman: Dar Al-Hamid.
- Alhazzayma, Mohammed, (1994), **Ideology and foreign policy: a comparative study**, Un published Ph.D. Dissertation, University of Tunisia, Tunisia.
- Alhlsa, Adib, (1971), **foundations of legislation and the judicial system in the Jordan**, Cairo: Institute of Research and Arab Studies.
- Al-hussein king Abdullah II. (1950). The memoirs of king Abdullah of Jordan, London.
- Al-Jamal, Yahya, (1970), **Contemporary Political System,** Cairo
- Al-Khatib, Anwar, (1970), **the state and the constitutional systems**, Edition2, Beirut.
- Al-Kilani, Farouk, (1966), **Special Courts in Jordan,** Edition1, Beirut.
- Al-Mashaqbeh, Ameen, (1988), **Political modernization and political stability in Jordan**, Amman: Dar aljeel, Beirut: Addar al arabeyeh.
- Al-Mashaqbeh, Amin, (2005), **National Education and the Jordanian political system**, Edition 7, Amman.
- Al-Mashaqbeh, Amin, (2006), **National Education,** Amman
- Al-Mashaqbeh, Amin, (2007), **parliament in Arab states**, Beirut.
- Area Handbook for H.K.J.(1969).
- Aruri Nasseer, (1972). Jordan Astudy in political development. Netherlands: martinus the Huge.
- Aruri,Nasser, ed, (1983), **Occupation: Israel Over Palestine,** Belmont. Mass: Association of Arab- American University Graduates, INC.
- Attia, Ahmed, (1972), **Political dictionary,** Renaissance House Press.
- Cord, Robert and Lawson, Kay, (1985), **The Human Polity,** Boston: Mass Press.

- Dioctyl, Raymond, (1963), **Political Science,** Part II, (translation of Fadel Zaki), Baghdad.
- El-Sayed Selim, Mohamed, (1984), **Foreign Policy Analysis**, Cairo: Professional Advertising agency.
- Hiyari, Adel, (1972), **Constitutional Law: Jordanian Political System,** Amman.
- Horiu, Andre, (1977), **Constitutional law and political institutions**.
- Huntington, Samuel (1974). Political order in changing societies, new have, yale unio press.
- Huntington, Samuel, (1968), **Political Order in Changing Societies,** New Haven: Yale University Press.
- Issa, Mahmoud and Ghali, Boutros, (1979), **An Entry to Political Science**, Cairo: The Anglo-Egyptian Bookshop.
- John King, Gainble Jr,. (1983), **Introduction to Political Science**.
- **Journal of the Arab world**, No.1176, 09/17/1999.
- King Hussein Bin Talal's speech in his address to form the charter committee, Amman, April 1990.
- **Knight magazine**, No.140, September 1999.
- Lent, James, (1990), **Hussein: biography**.
- Mahfouz, Abdel Moneim,(1987), **the principles of the political systems**, Amman.
- Mousa, Suleiman, (1968), **History of Jordan in the 20ᵗʰ Century,** Amman.
- Nyrop, Richard (1974). Area hand book for H.K.J, w,d,c,
- Obeidat,Ahmed, (1996), a lecture at the seminar of the National Charter, Amman, Royal Cultural Centre, June 1996.
- P.j. vatikiotis, (1957) political and military in Jordan (1921-1957) N.Y.
- Patai. Raphael (1958). The Hashemite kingdome of Jordan. N.Y.
- Ranney, Austin, (1975), **the Governing Of Men**, Illinois: Dryden Press
- Reese howard. (1969) Area hand book for H.K.J, Washington, D.c: Systems reaserch, corp,
- Said, Fouad, (1988), **Jordanian Foreign Policy: A Study of variables**, Un published Master Thesis, National Institute of Studies and Socialism, Baghdad.
- Shiha, Ibrahim, (1981), **contemporary political systems: state and governments**, Beirut.
- Shwadran, Benjamin, (1959), **Jordan, A State of Tension,** NY: Council for Middle Eastern Affairs Press.
- Shwadran, Jordan (1959). Astate of tension, N.Y, council of M.E affairs press.
- **The economic report**, Issue 42 June 1999.
- Vatikiotis, P.J., (1957), **Politics and Military in Jordan: (1921-1975),** N.Y: Frederic.A. Prager.

Author in brief Personal Information

Name: Amin Awwad Muhanna Al-Mashaqbeh.
Date of Birth: 12/11/1955.
Place of Birth: Al Mafraq / Jordan.

Qualifications:

- Ph.D. in political science / comparative politics, the University of Southern California (USC) / Los Angeles, United States, 1986, Dissertation title: MODERNIAZATION AND POLITICAL STABILITY AND INSTABILITY: The Jordanian Case, 1955-1986
- Masters of Comparative Politics / University of Southern California, Los Angeles, 1984.
- Masters of International Relations, Fairleigh Dickinson University, New Jersey, United States of America 1980.
- BA in Political Science /College of Commerce and Economics, University of Jordan, Amman, 1978.
- General secondary school, secondary school of Mafraq, Jordan,1974.

Rank:

Professor.

Government posts held:

- Minister for Social Development / Jordan 1991-1993
- Chairman of the Interim Committee of the General Federation of Charity 2007-2011.
- Chairman of Jordan Press and Publishing "Addustour" (Part-time) 2011 to present.
- Member of the Board of Higher Education and Vice President of the Council, 2009 to present

Academic and administrative expertise:

- Lecturer of Political Science, University of Yarmouk 1980-1982.
- Assistant Professor / Department of Political Science / Yarmouk University 1986-1991.
- Visiting Professor / University of Tennessee / Knoxville, United States, 1989.

- Assistant Dean of the Faculty of Arts and Humanities / Yarmouk University 1990-1991.
- Associate Professor of Political Science / Yarmouk University 1993-1996.
- Associate Professor of Political Science / University of Applied Sciences 1996-2000.
- Dean of public affairs, the Jordan Institute of Diplomacy summer 1998.
- Professor Emeritus / Jordan Institute of Diplomacy, Amman 1998-2002.
- Associate Professor Department of Political Science / Yarmouk University 2000 to 2002.
- Associate Professor in the Department of Political Science / Kuwait University 2002 -2003- 2004-2005.
- Professor/ Department of Political Science/ Yarmouk University 10/3/2003-9/9/2006.
- Expert and consultant in the preparation of a National Education teaching manual, Ministry of Education, Amman 2006.
- National Education expert, and citizen program, Minhaj Foundation, Amman / 2006.
- Adviser in the Arab Center for the Rule of Law and Integrity - Beirut, Lebanon.
- Expert and main author of participation and Arab parliaments, the Arab Center for the Rule of Law and Integrity - Beirut, Lebanon, 2006.
- Professor of Political Science University of the Middle East for Higher Studies - Amman, 2006-2010
- Expert and consultant in the preparation of the social science and National Education curriculum, 2006 - 2007. - Member Economic and Social Council 2007-2011.
- Vice Chairman of the Board of Trustees of the University of Mutah 2008-2009.
- Professor of Political Science Department of fundamental sciences, University of Jordan, 2010-2011 - 2012 to present.

Author's publications

1. Modernization and political stability in Jordan, Dar Al Jeel / Beirut, Lebanon, 1989.
2. Jordanian political system (facts and concepts) Dar Zahran / Amman, 1990.
3. Prince Shaker bin Zaid, upbringing and life (1934-1885) military presses Amman 1995.

4. National Education, the Jordanian political system and the democratic process, the first edition Dar al-Hamid, Amman 1996, 2nd ed. 1997.

5. Letters of His Royal Highness Prince Hassan, 1995, Editor, Amman 1997.

6. Hassan Bin Talal, visions and ideas in the development of democracy and peace, Ministry of Culture, Amman 1998.

7. National Education, the Jordanian political system and the democratic process, 3rd ed., 1998, 4th ed., 1999, Dar al-Hamid, Amman.

8. Jordanian foreign policy, reality and the aspirations, Editor, Amman 2000.

9. Jordanian Foreign Policy and neighboring countries, Editor, Amman 2000.

10. Jordanian political system and the democratic process, the fifth edition, Dar al-Hamid, Amman, 2000, Sixth Edition, 2002.

11. Jordanian Foreign Policy and the Gulf Cooperation Council (GCC), Editor, Dar al-Hamid, Amman, 2002.

12. Political reform in the Arab world, editor, Center for Strategic Studies, University of Kuwait 2005.

13. National Education, eighth edition, the Dar al-Hamid, Amman 2005.

14. Parliaments in Arab countries, Jordan, Egypt, Lebanon, Morocco, Beirut, 2007.

15. Jordanian political system, Greater Amman Minicipality, a cultural, Amman 2010.

16. Political reform and good governance, Dar al-Hamid, Amman 2010.

17. Security challenges for U.S. foreign policy in the Middle East, Amman, 2011.

18. Darfur geopolitical realities, conflict and future, Amman, 2011.

19. King and the three authorities, Amman, 2012

Scientific papers: 29 scientific papers published.